WOOD YOU BELIEVE

VOLUME ONE

THE UNFOLDING SELF

HEALING & SELF-AWARENESS
EXPLORING SPIRITUALITY AND PSYCHOLOGY
THROUGH HANDCRAFTED WOOD SYMBOLS

FR. JIM COGLEY

© 2005 FR. JIM COGLEY. All Rights Reserved.

No part of this book may be reproduced, stored in a retrieval system, or transmitted by any means without the written permission of the author.

First published by AuthorHouse 05/11/05

ISBN: 1-4208-1675-6 (sc)

1663 LIBERTY DRIVE
BLOOMINGTON, INDIANA 47403
(800) 839-8640
www.authorhouse.com

The message of this book is both profoundly simple, and simply profound.

OUR LIVES MAY BE PERFECTLY IMPERFECT, YET WE HAVE THE CAPACITY TO BE, PERFECTLY WHOLE.

*'Well got at'- A nature sculpture.
Perfectly imperfect, yet perfectly whole!
'Wood You Believe'*

This book is a companion volume to:

WOOD YOU BELIEVE
VOLUME TWO

THE EMERGING SELF

A JOURNEY OF SELF-DISCOVERY & HEALING
EXPLORING SPIRITUALITY AND PSYCHOLOGY
THROUGH HANDCRAFTED WOOD SYMBOLS

FR. JIM COGLEY

Acknowledgements

All the pieces illustrated in this book represent my own work done over a three-year period. The turned pieces were made with a Polewood 2000 lathe using hand-held tools. While many of the concepts are original, there are several that I have drawn from the work of other turners. These designs have been taken, and usually adapted, from a wide variety of sources such as books, exhibitions, and especially the magazine *Woodturning*. While I am deeply indebted to so many for their originality, it is impossible to always give credit where credit is due. I unreservedly apologize for any of these inadvertent omissions either with text or design and would welcome these being brought to my notice. One individual in particular, who through his books has inspired me greatly to expand the boundaries of conventional turning, is David Springett from Rugby in Warwickshire. Many of his intricate, unusual, and improbable designs form an integral part of this work, and to him I am most grateful, as master turner and mentor. To Nikos Siragas a wood-turner from Crete I am indebted for the original concepts of the Geni and Cobra vases. The original design of the Music Box belongs to S. Gary Roberts, and for the Clinging Vine design I am grateful to Chris Pye.

The stories included are factual and have arisen out of clinical and pastoral practice. In all cases names have been changed and details rearranged but in a manner that preserves their essential truth. For literary purposes they have also been shortened considerably and a story that may have taken months to unfold is now condensed into a short paragraph.

I am deeply grateful to all who have helped in preparing the material for this publication, especially; Tomás Hayes, Maria Colfer, Fr. Séamus de Val, Ann-Marie Ferris, Áine O Ceallaigh. Their advice and support has been invaluable.

Extracts from the writings of Herman Hesse on trees are from *Wandering*, translated by James Wright.

The piece from John O'Donoghue's book *Anam Chara* is reprinted by permission of The Random House Group Ltd. and published by Bantam Books.

The cover piece of Volume One entitled *The Unfolding Self* is an original design by the author. It is made from sycamore, purple-heart and banksai nut. 'Individuation' was the term coined by Carl Jung for the process of becoming whole or one's own unique person. Here the true Self that is always trying to emerge is given symbolic expression.

Proceeds from this work go towards the sponsorship of children in poor countries.

The Unfolding Self - Wood You Believe, Copyright © 2005 by James P. Cogley.
All rights reserved. No part of this publication may be reproduced, stored in a retrieval system, or transmitted in any form or by any means, electronic, mechanical, photocopying or otherwise, without the prior permission of the copyright owner.

WOOD YOU BELIEVE – Volume One
THE UNFOLDING SELF

Table of Contents

Acknowledgements vii

                A tree says   xiii

Introduction xv
    Possibilities Awaken xv
    Discovery and Integration xv
    Trees of Life xvi

1   **Images of God** 1
    Divine Perspectives 1
    The Creator's perspective 1
    Infinite Patience 2
    Acceptance – The Key to Moving Forward 3

2   **Self-Acceptance and Self-Esteem** 5
    Where do I Begin? 5
    If my Life were a Building 5
    How do I Define Myself? 5
    Embraced by the Truth 6
    The Trick of Balance 9
    Indications of a Healthy Self-Image 10
    Self-Empowering 11
    Where are You? 11
    Who am I? 12

                A tree says   xiii

3   **The Ties that Bind** 14
    Claiming our Identity 14
    Hating and Separating 15
    The trouble with being a Perfect Child 16
    A Devouring Mother Love 17
    A Love Triangle 17
    Misogynist Alert! 18
    Father of a Multitude 19

		The Father Wound	19
4	**The Inner Child**		21
		Parenting our Lost Self	21
		Who/What is the Inner Child?	22
		The Long Journey Home	24
		Seeking the Lost	24
		Changing our Perceptions	24
		A Parenting Story	25
5	**The Masks We Wear**		27
		Becoming Real	27
		Envy – A Betrayal of Self	28
6	**Featuring Defects**		30
		The Stone Rejected	30
		A Feature is an Accepted Defect	30
		A Past Revisited	32
		Perfectly Imperfect	34
		Perfectly Whole	34
7	**Mistakes and Remakes**		36
		The Long and Winding Road	36
		The Jericho Road	37
		The Cul-de-Sac of Remorse	37
		Taking Responsibility	37
		Guilt and Shame	39
8	**Befriending Shadow**		41
		The Dark Side of Self	41
		'Be You Perfect' ~~ 'Be Perfectly You'	42
		Accepting the seemingly Unacceptable	44
		Unmasking the Shadow of Inferiority	44
		Shadow Projections and Relationships	44
		The Stranger and the Estranged	45
9	**Mirror Image**		47
		As Within so Without	47
		Mirroring Relationships	48
		Inner Reality affecting Outer Reality	49
		A Timely Reminder	51

10	**Forgiven and Forgiving**	52
	The Road to Freedom	52
	Guilt and Resentment	53
	Grievances – The Unhappy ever after Saga	54
	How do I Forgive?	54
11	**The Suffering Self**	56
	It's Yew – It's You!	56
12	**Treasure from the Deep**	59
	Transforming the Unacceptable	59
	Advice from an Angel	62
13	**Getting a Balance**	64
	Being and Doing	64
	Personality Types	66
	Mid-Life Balance	66
14	**Embracing Assertiveness**	68
	A Matter of Respect	68
	The Passive Aggressive	73
15	**Birth Scripts – Life Scripts**	75
	What Was or What Is?	75
	Birth Legacies	75
	Rebirth	76
16	**Transformation of the Self**	79
	Collective Expectations	80
	The Primary Vocation – Called to be Myself	81
17	**True Self or False Self**	83
	Thermometer or Thermostat?	83
	Grace – Effortless Power	87
18	**The Kingdom Within**	88
	The Hidden Treasure of the Self	88
	Individuation – Becoming Who I really Am	89
Selected Bibliography for Volume one and Two		91
About the Author		95

Trees are sanctuaries,
Whoever knows how to speak to them, whoever knows how to listen to them,
can learn the truth.
They do not preach learning and precepts,
They preach undeterred by particulars,
the ancient law of life.
A tree says 'a kernel is hidden in me',
A spark, a thought,
I am life from eternal life.
The attempt and the risk that
the eternal mother took
With me is unique.
Unique the form and veins of my skin.
Unique the smallest play of leaves
in my branches,
and the smallest scar on my back.
I was made to form and reveal the eternal,
in my smallest special detail.

HERMAN HESSE

Introduction

Possibilities Awaken

Growing up on a farm, where there was an abundance of trees, meant that much of my childhood was spent high in the branches. Working with wood appealed to me greatly and to pursue a career in woodworking was something I considered, but felt called instead to a life in Ministry. For the next twenty-five years my budding love affair with wood was all but forgotten. Christmas of '98, I preached a sermon which was to have a profound impact on my life and rekindle that long forgotten passion. The topic chosen was, 'Christmas as the Birth of Possibilities'. I mentioned that it's all too easy to look at the impact that Christ's life had on the world but at the same time to forget about the possibilities and potential of our own lives. Just how I was going to put into practice what I was preaching was a question at the back of my mind. As if in answer, I heard a little voice say, 'Go to the wood'. As a belated Christmas present to myself, I then bought a lathe and a few chisels, and with a freshly cleaned out garage embarked on one of the most fulfilling and amazing adventures of my life. The first six months I now look back on as a frenzy of learning and production with every available free moment spent turning. Even sleep was sacrificed on the altar of the lathe. By June wooden objects of all descriptions had appeared like mushrooms in my living room and an exhibition was necessary, if for no other reason than just to create space. Thankfully that was almost a sellout and the £4,000 raised was able to go towards the education of children who had been orphaned because of AIDS in Uganda. That in turn became a catalyst for a local charity to be formed that still exists and raises thousands each year in support of this worthy cause.

Discovery and Integration

The next phase of work, which I like to term 'Discovery and Integration', continues to the present day and hopefully will remain for as long as I have days. As a priest my background was in spirituality, psychotherapy and counselling. To the latter I had given four years of training, and nearly twenty-five years of practice. The age-old dichotomy between these two disciplines was one that had always left me feeling uncomfortable. Surely spirituality and psychology were just different aspects of the one great reality and they should never be split. Only by taking them together could they help us fully to embody our spirit, to fulfill our potential and to reclaim our wholeness. I was quite aware that much of the earlier psychology was soulless without any awareness of, or even openness to, the spiritual dimension. This left it very limited and only able to provide a fleeting shadow of our full reality. At the same time I was also very wary of spiritual paths that tried to bypass our humanity. Much of the spirituality I had grown up with, and had been taught, seemed to ignore the shadow side of human nature. It encouraged us to suppress our emotions and desires, and it regarded the body as an encumbrance to the spirit. What I was searching for was a psycho-spiritual approach to everyday life which would bridge the gap between psychology and spiritual practice, where personality and soul, darkness and light, matter and spirit, our hearts of gold and our feet of clay could be embraced as different aspects of what it means to be a 'whole' or 'wholesome' human being. In earlier years my model of spirituality had been to strive for perfection, now this had changed dramatically into a quest for wholeness and integration'.

It was while working with the lathe, and exploring my own creativity, that I began to make the exciting discovery that many of the insights I had gleaned over the years were there, plain to be seen, in trees and wood in a manner that integrated both disciplines. In the pages that follow, it is difficult to say whether many of these insights are spiritual or psychological in nature. This may be a very welcome development, and due in no small measure to the fact that they are presented through wood. The wonder of trees and the beauty of wood bring together that which otherwise could be seen as quite diverse.

Trees of Life

Trees are the oldest, the tallest, and the largest living organisms on this earth. For millions of years, before the dawn of humanity, trees reigned supreme. They generously provide us with their basic ingredient that from the cradle to the grave is our constant companion. Almost every stage of our lives we can associate with wood. Just to look around and become aware of the number of things made from wood that we use and take for granted in our everyday lives, is in itself to evoke a profound act of gratitude for this most friendly and humble of materials. As children we are placed in a wooden cot, at school we sit in a wooden desk, we eat off wooden tables, walk on wooden floors, sit at a wood fire. In infinitely unnoticed ways it supports and enriches our lives. We greatly admire its diversity and beauty. For many, it is a means of livelihood, and after a lifetime of association with this most versatile of substances, our bodies are placed in a wooden box. We humans have no greater ally on this planet that we call home.

Because trees are alive, and wood is an organic material, human beings often identify the struggle of trees for survival with their own survival story. In so many ways trees seem to mirror aspects of our lives and have their own personalities. The memory of each season's growth and the length of years is captured in the annual rings. Even the irregular outline of their trunks reminds us of the uncertain nature of life. Humans too have looked to trees to feed their spirit. It was beneath a tree that the Buddha received enlightenment. In the Judaeo-Christian tradition it was as a result of eating the fruit of a forbidden tree that Adam and Eve were exiled from the Garden of Eden. It was on the wood of a tree that Christ the Saviour died.

This book came about after twenty-five years of preaching, teaching, counselling and giving seminars on many of the subjects covered in these pages. It is written in the hope that many of the insights which I have gleaned from listening to others, and through much personal searching and struggle, will be as beneficial to readers as they have been to me. Much of what can be read in a sentence may have taken many years of blood, sweat and tears to discover. Perhaps that is how it is with wisdom, once discovered: it appears so obvious, yet the discovery itself is often painful and tedious.

While there is already a multitude of self-help books now available, much more work is needed in the area of exploring the relationship between psychology and spirituality. With my own background, and particular interest in trees and woodturning, I believe that it is possible to make a significant contribution, particularly through the use of this medium. To the best of my knowledge, this approach of attempting to integrate spirituality and psychology and present a journey of healing through the medium of wood may never before have been attempted, and certainly not to any significant degree. From that perspective this book could be quite unique.

The following pages represent a very personal journey with wood, where we will allow it to speak to us about some of the mysteries of life, and of our own existence. As we listen to its secrets we will be invited to reflect on our lives in a manner which will give them greater meaning and purpose. Like the tree, which often hides its beauty beneath a crusty bark we will be invited to discover our own inner beauty and riches. St. Irenaeus from the early Christian era is still remembered for his statement that, 'The glory of God is man fully alive'. Allowing trees and wood to speak to us in a manner that facilitates the unfolding of our true Self, and in the process become more fully human and fully alive, is what this book is all about.

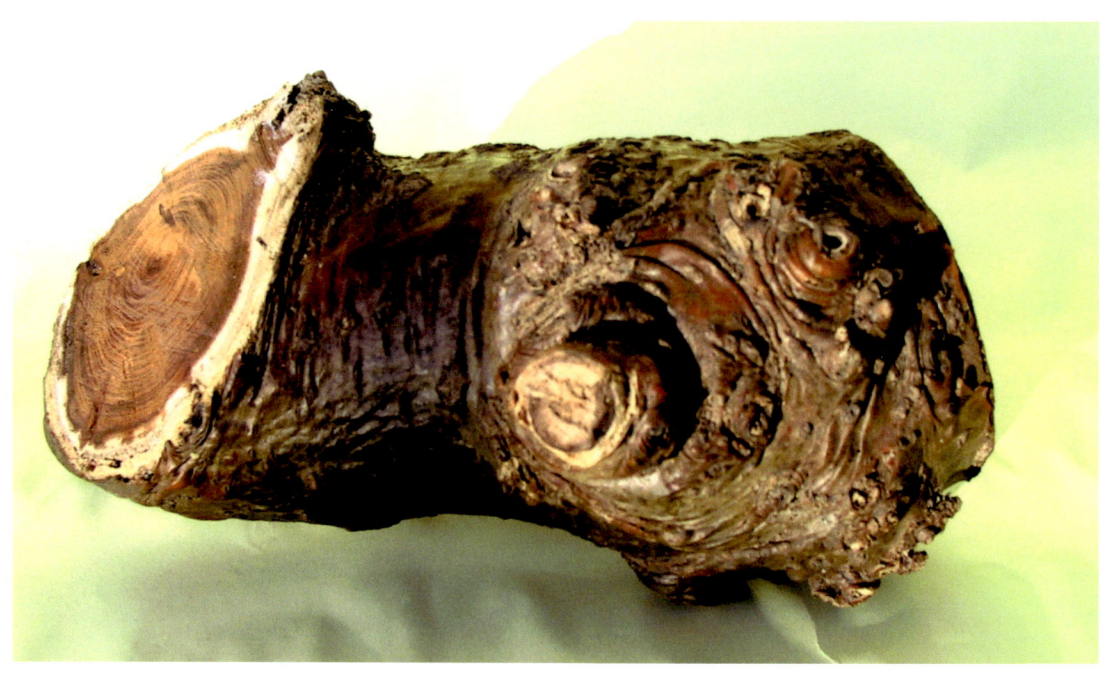

The Raw Material

A Piece of Wood

By Henry Rohr

Every possibility is sleeping in such a piece of wood
It depends on you
how you look at it
what you see in it-

some useless obstacle in your way
fuel to light your fire
material
to build a fence around your isolation
to build a house – a door – a table.

OR a challenge
Waiting just for you
To be set free
To be called to life.

The woodcarver, the artist sees it like that.
He takes it in his hands
And sees the hidden life
And makes it speak
Of growth and death
Joy and pain
And all the mysteries of life.

All this is contained in a piece of wood.

Our whole life
The world around us
Is like such a piece of wood.
It depends on us,
How we look at it, what we see in it.
Shouldn't we all be artists?

Images of God

Divine Perspectives

Carl Jung, the famous Swiss psychiatrist, was once asked, after a lifetime of psychological research, what his greatest discovery about human nature was. He replied that it was projection. This is the tendency to see in others what we are blind to in ourselves. Seeing the splinter in another's eye while being blind to the plank that is in our own is perhaps its best known Biblical expression. The character trait we most intensely dislike in someone else and what evokes a hostile reaction from us is most likely to be a carefully hidden and unacknowledged aspect of ourselves. This trait of projection even carries through into our relationship with God.

The image we have of God is something that profoundly affects our view of reality and how we live our lives. The Genesis story tells us that we are made in the image and likeness of God. Much of our difficulty begins when we start making God into our image and likeness; in other words, when we make God into a projection of ourselves. It is not uncommon for someone who is harsh, judgmental and unforgiving towards themselves to see God in a similar light, as a God of punishment. It is all too easy to project the unforgiving attitude I may have towards myself onto the Almighty. Many of the most common images are in fact projections. Someone who lives by the law and is legalistic in nature often holds a policeman image of a God who is always out to catch us breaking the rules. The idea of God as an old man with a white beard who stands at the balustrades of Heaven and is displeased at seeing his children having fun is often the lot of those with a puritanical disposition for whom pleasure has little space in their lives. One of my most memorable descriptions came from a woman who described God as someone whose expectations of her were so high, and whose opinion of her was so low, that she always felt she was living under his frown. At one level she was saying what her father had been like, now as an adult, having internalized that relationship, it was a description of her own inner world and it was now being projected onto God.

The Creator's Perspective

In common with most people of my age group, I belong to a generation who like so many before were more driven by the fear of God than drawn by his love. Working with wood has helped me enormously in transforming this image, particularly by identifying with God as Creator. From the Genesis account of creation we see God at each stage proudly looking at the work of his hands and seeing that is was all 'good'. For so many there is a very real difficulty in seeing ourselves in that light as 'good'. A woman who had survived an abusive childhood and led a wayward life was leaving a counselling session when the counsellor placed her hand on her shoulder and said, 'I hope you know that you really are a good person'. For the next two weeks that lady cried for joy. It was as if she had forgotten, and needed to be reminded of the greatest and most important truth of her life.

Again and again I have looked at a finished piece, the work of my hands, and felt a great sense of pride, satisfaction and achievement. At a deeper level I have sensed a divine truth, that the Lord too is proud of his creation. Just as an artist wouldn't dream of despising the work of his hands, so too He despises nothing of what he creates. With our innate tendency to see ourselves as unworthy and below par it is utterly liberating to take on board such wonderful Scriptural truths like those expressed in the Book of Psalms when the Lord says that He delights in us, that He is pleased with us, or that he rejoices over us as a bridegroom rejoices in his bride.

A Time for Celebration

Infinite Patience

On occasions, having invested a considerable amount of time on a particular piece, I have noticed that there is a direct correlation between the amount of time spent and the sense of satisfaction enjoyed. The greater the time investment, the greater is the reward. In the timescale of evolution the human species is a very late arrival. If that time frame were compared to a twenty-four hour clock, humanoids would only occupy the space of the last few seconds. Like the early Biblical writers who wrote of God in a very human way, I like to think of God longing for the high point of his great evolutionary plan, ecstatic at our eventual arrival, and still waiting for us to fully grasp the wonder of our creation and of our true identity. Viewed in this context, humans may be the high point of creation but our personal evolution is ongoing. At this point in history we have scaled the highest mountains, explored the deepest oceans, split the atom and put men on the moon. Perhaps after all the external challenges have been met, the greatest challenge still waits; to evolve in spiritual awareness and inhabit the reality of who we really are. To use a phrase from St. Paul to the Romans, (8:19) 'God still waits in eager longing for the revealing of his sons and daughters'.

Acceptance – The Key to Moving Forward

Acceptance and the Game of Life

The piece in the center showing two hands holding a sphere is entitled 'Acceptance'. On both the vase made of yew and the mahogany bowl are the emblems found on a pack of cards; hearts, diamonds, clubs and spades. There is undoubtedly a chance element in the game of life and the age-old saying, 'Life is like a hand of cards; it's how you play them that matters', carries a profound depth of wisdom. We cannot always choose what happens us in life but we do have a choice about how we respond to whatever happens. What is one person's meat can be another's poison. An Eastern mystic was once asked what was the secret of eternal laughter. He replied, 'The joyful acceptance of all that is'. In the Christian tradition, the equivalent can be found in the Pauline Epistles, 'In all situations give thanks, for this is the will of God' (Ephesians 5:20). The advice given is not easy, yet it does point the way forward. Growing up I recall being amazed at my parent's invariable response of, 'Blessed be the will of God' when things of an unwelcome or even tragic nature occurred. At the time I can often remember thinking that it couldn't be the will of a loving God. What sort of God would allow this to happen? Now with adult eyes I can appreciate the wisdom, so much a part of earlier generations, that such a response was a profound act of acceptance that enabled people, caught in the grip of tragedy, to move on with their lives. The opposite of acceptance is to indulge in resentment and engage in self-pity. Such a response is to remain a victim of circumstances, to live in the past and to become entombed in bitterness.

The power and wisdom of acceptance is captured in the words of a 12th-century Persian mystic and poet, Jalaluddin Rumi:

'Pain only exists in resistance.
Joy exists only in acceptance.
Painful situations which you heartily accept become joyful.
Joyful situations which you do not accept become painful.
There is no such thing as a bad experience.
Bad experiences are simply the creations of your resistance to
what is.'

One of the recipients of the Irish Persons of the Year Award in 2002 was a young woman named Caroline Casey who as a girl became almost totally blind. In spite of her disability she travelled through India on an elephant, engaged in all sorts of adventurous pursuits, and continues to raise large amounts of money for charity. The message of hope that she carries for all who have been dealt a difficult hand in life is timeless. Its essence is:

'Life is not fair, it's not always just, and it's certainly not easy, but if we gratefully embrace it with both hands then we can have a lot of fun and enjoy a very fulfilling life'.

In a nutshell we can say that gratitude is the attitude that sets the altitude for living.

2

Self-Acceptance and Self-Esteem

Where do I Begin?

Self-Esteem is the measure of how we feel about ourselves, how much we accept ourselves, believe in ourselves and see ourselves to be worthwhile. It is intrinsically linked to our self-image, and is related to self-confidence and self-respect.

The vast majority of people, if asked which were the most important relationships in their lives, would reply that it was their partner, parents, children or friends. Few would say that it was their relationship with themselves. Yet this is truly the most important relationship; all others come from it and are influenced by it. How I relate to myself is the single most determining factor in how I relate to others, to life and to God. Ultimately I cannot be closer to another human being than I am to myself. Whether I relate to myself as my own best friend or as my worst enemy is going to affect the quality of my life down to the very last detail. When asked what was the greatest of all the commandments, Jesus replied, 'You must love God with all your heart and your neighbour as yourself' (Matthew 22:37). In the history of Christian religious practice there has probably been no word so overlooked than that word *as*. The basic truth is that as I relate to myself so I will relate to others and to God.

If My Life were a Building!

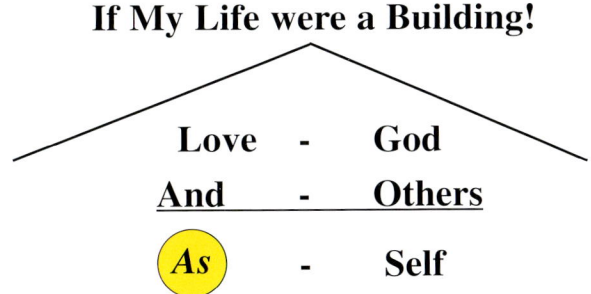

The relationship with Self forms the foundation for the building that constitutes my life. Cracks that appear in terms of relationship problems or faith crises may be temporarily plastered over, but as they continually widen out and reappear I eventually must accept that the real problem lies within the foundation. Weaknesses that manifest themselves in other areas of my life ultimately come from here, and can't be properly dealt with until they are tackled at source.

How do I Define Myself?

There is a very real tendency to fall into the ego trap of thinking that in order to be lovable we have to meet certain conditions. That we have to have a certain kind of body, to have gone to college, have money, have a good job, be of certain social status, be in a relationship, be successful and so on. Many of these are noble things to strive for, but the truth is that they have nothing to do with our Self-love and Self-worth. Just as a new born baby has a value and is lovable, even though it is totally incapable of earning that worth, so each one of us is of enormous value based purely on who we are, and not on what we do or fail to do. Another useful metaphor is to think of oneself as a diamond that has become coated in mud. The problem is that when we think of ourselves we see only the mud, often to the extent of completely overlooking the diamond underneath. The basic truth of Christianity is that we are God's children, we are loved totally, unconditionally and the diamond, which we are, is of inestimable worth.

Embraced by the Truth

The central meaning of the Incarnation is that God, by becoming Man, has divinely embraced us in the fullness of our humanity. This also implies that our journey to God invites us to fully enter into and accept all that it means to be human.

The piece shown is deeply symbolic and entitled 'The Embrace'. The sphere is a universal symbol of wholeness and totality. Throughout this book it is used to represent both who we are and what we can be. The enfolding feature tries to capture the idea of mutual embrace. First, God embracing us with all the frailty of our humanity, in His everlasting arms and then our need to embrace our full, human reality in unconditional love and acceptance.

The Embrace

In the discipline of woodturning, it is a simple but profound truth that before any work of transformation can begin on the lathe, the piece must first be accepted. The acceptance of 'Self' at the personal level also forms the basis for psychological transformation and growth. If sin is understood as 'that which divides' then the basis of all sin is 'Self-rejection'.

One of the great spiritual masters, teachers and writers of our age was the Jesuit priest Anthony de Mello. At his last retreat given shortly before his untimely death he spoke the following words that in many ways reflected his view of how change takes place in our lives.

Don't Change,
Trying to change is the enemy of love.
Don't change yourself,
accept yourself as you are.
Don't change others,
accept them as they are.
Don't change the world,
It's in God's hands.
If you do that,
then change will occur,
marvellously, miraculously,
in its own way,
and in its own time.
Just yield to the current of life,
unencumbered by baggage.

Anthony De Mello

From the Book of Sirach (10:27 & 28) comes a very pertinent piece of advice concerning how we should relate to ourselves:

> 'With humility have self-esteem.
> Prize yourself as you deserve.
> Who can acquit the one who condemns himself?
> Who can lift up the person who puts himself down'?

Likewise the Buddha expressed a similar truth when he told his followers:

> 'You may travel the whole world and you will find no one
> more in need of the alms of your own compassion than yourself'.

In more recent times, as modern psychology has recognized the age-old truth of the importance of being in right relationship with oneself, the Swiss psychologist Carl Jung drew attention to the passage of Scripture in St. Matthew's Gospel that speaks of the Last Judgment. Here the 'sheep' are rewarded and the 'goats' are punished on the basis of how they treated the 'least of the brethren'. This involved giving food to the hungry, drink to the thirsty, clothing the naked, welcoming the stranger, visiting those sick or imprisoned. The 'least of the brethren' he suggests has always been interpreted in Christian teaching as referring to others in their time of need, but it could also be looked on as referring to ourselves. Hence his big question: 'What if at the end of the day the Lord were to say to any of us, but you were the least of the brethren, and how did you treat yourself?'

The Trick of Balance

Balancing Egg

The piece depicted is a balancing egg that is really a piece of trickery. Inside the egg is a ball bearing that has to be centered in the recess at the top in order for the egg to balance. Just a slight movement and it falls into the off-centre groove and the next person to attempt the balancing act is attempting the impossible. It is unfortunate that 'self- centredness' has been understood as egocentricity when in fact it is essential for psychological maturity. If we are off centre with ourselves then how can we be on centre with others?

For so many it is very difficult to achieve a healthy selfish / selfless balance. To be selfish is to care for ourselves and look after our own needs without feeling guilty, and to be selfless is to reach out to others in love, to give of ourselves freely and generously without feeling resentful.

Indications of a healthy Self-Image

People who accept themselves will generally be:

- Able to go out to others easily and unselfconsciously.
- Able to be their real selves and not hide behind a mask.
- Able to be assertive and express their own opinions.
- Able to face conflict and handle it constructively.
- Able to take responsibility for their actions.

- Able to give and receive compliments.
- Able to stand on their own two feet and be interdependent with others.
- Able to make mistakes without feeling destroyed.
- Able to relate more than react.
- Able to adopt to change without feeling threatened.
- Able to appreciate and learn from constructive criticism.
- Able to receive graciously and give generously.
- Able to express their true feelings.
- Able to be internally directed and not depend on external authority.
- Able to be non-judgmental and accepting of others.

Self-Empowering

If there are two keys to psychological and spiritual health then unconditional self-love is one and reclaiming our personal power is the other. Most of us have inherited a legacy of low self-esteem with the result that the power that we are lacking in ourselves we give to others. The extent to which another person has the power to cause me upset or make me lose my peace of mind is a good indication of how much power I have given away. It is all too easy to see how our lack of self-identity becomes suffused in others, when in response to the question who we are, we define ourselves as so and so's wife, husband or parent, brother, sister or friend. A further extension of this happens when we define ourselves in terms of the work we do, the possessions we have or the size of our bank balance. Finding our identity in terms of someone or something, other than who we really are, is to give that person or thing an enormous power over us. This has to be reclaimed if we are to live fully the life that is ours.

Where are You?

The first question in the Bible, 'Adam, where are you?' (Genesis 3:9), is still as relevant today as it was when first posed. For so many, it is a very difficult question to answer. It is not that they have a conflictual relationship with themselves, but rather that they have no connection at all. The world of external realities has become so absorbing and time consuming that there's no room left in the picture for the deeper Self.

Betty was a woman in her early fifties, suffering from depression. Her five children and her husband, she said, were her whole life. The children were now at the stage where they were leaving the nest and making their own lives. This was something she was finding very difficult to cope with and seemed to have triggered her depression. When asked did she ever consider herself, she replied 'I don't. For years I have been so busy being mother that I have never once thought of myself!' Such a scenario of the dutiful, self-sacrificing mother is all too common. Her identity becomes lost in her family, with the result that their going away is extremely difficult for all parties and for the mother it is felt as if she is losing herself.

For this woman her journey of recovery began with the awareness of what her depression was trying to say; that she had lived her life through her family and now her deeper Self was crying out for recognition. At first she found it very uncomfortable spending time alone but she persevered knowing that creating space for herself was so important. She also began to practice meditation and discovered that the half hour she gave to this each day was the key element in transforming her life and allowing her to discover who she was from within, rather than from without as she had been doing for so many years.

Who am I?

Once upon a time a woman was recovering from a serious illness. She dreamt that she had died and was met by an angel who asked her who she was. 'I am the wife of the mayor of my town', she replied. The angel answered, 'I didn't ask whose wife you were, I asked, who are you?' Again she replied ' I am the mother of six wonderful children'. Again the angel replied, 'I didn't ask whose mother you are, I asked, who are you?' Again she replied, 'I am a committed Christian who attends church regularly and I am very charitable towards those in need'. Yet again the angel replied, 'I didn't ask what religion you belonged to or what good you do, I asked, who are you?' After seven attempts she woke up but still hadn't answered the question. The rest of her life was spent in search of the answer.

Self Acceptance and Self Esteem

A tree says:
My strength is trust.
I know nothing about my fathers.
I know nothing about the thousand children
that every year spring out of me.
I live out the secret of my seed
To the very end,
And I care for nothing else.
I trust that God is in me.
I trust that my labour is holy.
Out of this trust I live

HERMAN HESSE

3

The Ties that Bind

Claiming our Identity

One of the most amazing paradoxes in the teaching of Christ is where He, on one hand, advocates love of neighbour as self, and, at the same time says, 'If someone were to come after me without hating father, mother, wife, brothers, sisters and his own life too he cannot be my disciple' (Luke 14:26). The word 'hate' is very strong and seems to totally negate the main thrust of his teaching about the primacy of love. Viewed from a psychological perspective, such a strong term makes perfect sense. It displays a profound insight into the make-up of human nature. It expresses what is necessary if maturity is to be achieved, and how the path of discipleship is to be embraced.

'Hating' here can be understood as the necessary prelude to genuinely loving someone as opposed to merely needing them. As long as our identity is found outside ourselves there is a very real possibility that our need will masquerade as love. The other person, instead of feeling the love which we might adamantly express, may instead feel trapped by our neediness. To actually hate, albeit temporarily, may be necessary for stifling dependency to give way to healthy inter-dependency, where power is reclaimed and identity is confirmed.

Fig. 1 **Mother and Child**

Fig. 2 **Emancipation**

Hating and Separating

The two night-lights depicted in fig. 1 and fig. 2 with the sea urchin shells provide a useful illustration of the importance of 'hating' and 'separating'. The first is called 'Mother and Child'. The child in the early stages has no identity apart from its mother. Gradually it begins to move away from mother and take on its own form and identity. At some stage there has to be a final severance of the umbilical cord in order for the child to be its own unique person and for its own personality to shine forth. This means that while the child must gradually claim its freedom, the mother must also be prepared to let go. Where there is a tendency to hold on by either party a certain amount of pain and suffering is inevitable and absolutely necessary for psychological maturity to take place. In fig. 1 the small urchin finds its light from the larger shell, the child is still an extension of its mother, while in fig. 2 the severance is complete, light comes from within and personal identity is now expressed in exquisite beauty. At the wider level whenever our identity is invested outside ourselves and where our own power is lacking, despite how radical it sounds, we may need to 'hate' before we can reclaim what is really ours and come into the expression of who we really are. Letting go is usually a prelude to actually having. Before a bond of pure love can be established quite a lot of painful separation may be necessary.

The Trouble with being a 'Perfect' Child

When a young person enters the rebellious stage of adolescence and is not getting their own way, he or she may well say to the parents in a fit of rage, 'I hate you' or, 'I don't like you'. It takes a very mature parent to take such a blow on the chin without retaliating or feeling deeply hurt, but instead to appreciate the underlying significance of such a remark. Without the child causing this necessary hurt there is a real danger that they will never claim their own identity but always remain at some level fused with the parent. It is a paradox that it is often the 'perfect' young person who has never caused the parents a moment's trouble that ends up most troubled themselves. One rather enlightened mother who was told by her daughter, 'Mummy, I really don't like you', replied; 'Darling there are times when I don't like you very much either in the way you behave, but I never stop loving you'.

The reasons why the umbilical cord may never have been fully severed are many and varied. They include such factors as:

Rejection in the womb, unwanted pregnancy, attempted abortion.

Separation from the mother shortly after birth.

Mother having suffered from Post Natal Depression.

Child expected to fill the mother's need for love.

Over protective mother arising from her own hurt childhood.

Death of previous child, and the next is then expected to compensate for the loss.

Lack of bonding after birth, e.g. mother very ill.

Mother unable to give adequate nurturance to the child.

Any significant separation from mother in early period, e.g. prolonged stay in hospital.

Mother being emotionally unavailable to child, e.g. as in grief.

Child acting as a buffer between mother and abusive father.

Mother holding on to her identity as mother for too long and refusing to let go.

Too much control and dominance from mother where she holds all the power.

Child/Adult choosing to remain emotionally dependent.

Lack of male influence to help the natural separation process.

Death of mother before the child reaches maturity.

One of the most common reasons why separation is never completed is where the mother unconsciously wants to hold on to her identity as mother. This takes the form of not giving her offspring the freedom necessary to find his or her own identity. The telltale signs that this may be happening is where the mother continues to do for her child what he or she is capable of doing for himself or herself. At a surface level this makes her appear as the good and dutiful mother while the unconscious dynamics at work mean that the child remains dependent and never grows up. Since dependent children find it very difficult to separate, her identity as mother remains intact. Where this happens in the case of a son, he is very likely to marry his mother in the guise of another woman. His wife on the other hand ends up adopting a son when in fact she thought she was marrying a husband. A co-dependent relationship is formed which may or may not survive the passage of time, but will remain incapable of delivering the happiness and fulfillment that only a mature relationship can bring. The Scriptural injunction that in order to be married 'a man must leave father and mother in order to be joined to his wife', may have been physically fulfilled, in the sense of leaving home, but the deeper psychological bond, being allowed to remain intact, means that the marriage is being undermined from the start.

A Devouring Mother Love

Agnes first came in her late seventies to talk about the problems she was having with her 'children' who I discovered ranged in age from forty to sixty years old! She had reared twelve, each one more dysfunctional than the other. Their problems included criminal activity, addictions, domestic violence and a host of others. All of these ensured that they were never out of trouble. In their hour of need they always arrived on mother's doorstep where they always knew they would find shelter and support. Her word was law and she was the undisputed matriarch. While apparently suffering greatly because of their many misdemeanours, it became clear after a number of chats that at a deeper level everything was not as it seemed on the surface. In fact Agnes needed her 'children' to be constantly in the wars and she was secretly delighted that they always came back to her in times of crisis. If they were not so dependent she would see far less of them. Because of a deep insecurity she was desperately clinging to her identity as mother. One could postulate that even as they were being reared her offspring had been programmed into being problematic so that they would always remain dependent and never have to grow up. When Agnes died her identity as 'mother' was still very much intact and her helpless 'children' mourned intensely for the one who was the only 'rock' in their lives.

A Love Triangle

Roy was reared by his elder sister from age three until he was seven. He remembered longing for his mother and seeking attention by being disruptive. His first serious female relationship was very dependent where he allowed her to be in control and do everything for him. After some years of living together he began to treat her badly and she left him. Years later, and in another this time very healthy relationship, he was deeply puzzled that he still couldn't let go of the first. His partner felt that she was competing with an invisible third party and couldn't take it any more. The realization that the first relationship had been operating at the child-parent level made him see that it was the young child in him that was still yearning for his mother and not allowing him to enjoy a full adult-adult relationship until its needs were first looked after.

Symptoms of Negative Bond to Mother

Lack of personal identity
Irrational mood swings
Poor sense of personal boundaries
Addictive behaviour
Anger/Depression
Overeating/Undereating/Food allergies
Sexual dysfunction
Attraction to dangerous pursuits
Heart problems

Carrier of other people's feelings
Over sensitive/Pleaser mentality
Search for our own space
Childish behaviour pattern
Easily gives power to others
Fear of rejection
Co-dependent relationships
Blocked creativity
Resisting change
Seeing nothing wrong with a dysfunctional relationship
Ambivalence towards female partner
Needing extreme closeness and apartness
Tendency towards violence
Suicidal thoughts
Homo- or bi-sexuality in male
Mental fuzziness/lack of clarity
Obscured sense of direction
Observer of life more than participator
Separation Anxiety
Irresponsible tendencies
Susceptible to emotional blackmail

Misogynist Alert!

There can be little doubt that the greatest and most difficult task for every male is complete separation from the mother. The extent of power or control he allows subsequent females to have over him is ample evidence of this. Misogyny, the term used for a hatred of the female, is a condition far more widespread than is generally recognized. The male who has not dealt with his maternal bond will have a deep underlying anger towards his mother for not being free and this will inevitable be displaced onto subsequent women in his life. For a woman, a misogynist is initially a most beguiling creature. His need of the feminine is so great that he will appear as the perfect man, the fulfillment of all her dreams. He will most likely come across as charming, delightful, generous and sensual. Only as the relationship progresses, and commitments have been made, will the cracks begin to appear. Gradually her freedom to be her own person will begin to diminish, where she goes, what she does, whom she associates with, become matters that are always under scrutiny. Usually she tries to bend over backwards in order to please and even thinks that there must be something wrong with her when she can't succeed in making him happy. More and more she feels controlled by her partner's moods, and his anger either silent or expressed, backs her into a corner. As her world gets smaller, her self confidence diminishes and she feels trapped, unable to break free, or stand up for her own rights. Sensing her powerlessness the male will often turn more hostile and she may well feel as if she is being punished for something she hasn't done and as someone that she is not. These feelings are in fact quite accurate and reflect the truth. At the deepest level it is the male who feels controlled by the feminine and now that he has got the upper hand his revenge may come under many guises. In extreme cases this may take the form of beatings and rape. He may openly flaunt other women, indulge in pornography, deprive her financially, tell her that she's ugly and convince her that nobody else would want her. His deepest fear is that she will in fact leave him and this she may well have to do if she is to maintain her own sanity. In claiming her own freedom she is also indirectly offering him a lifeline to deal with his mother issues, for as long as she remains where he wants her to be he will never have to face himself.

Father of a Multitude

The need for a father to claim his own identity apart from that of being father is expressed in the Abraham saga in Genesis 22. Here God puts Abraham to the ultimate test by asking him to sacrifice his son Isaac. The prelude to the story is that God called Abraham at the age of seventy-five to leave his own country and to set out for a land that he would show him. Later God promised that he would give him a son through whom he would become the father of a multitude. When Abraham was eighty-five, God still had not fulfilled his promise and he and his wife Sarai were still childless. Abraham then decided that before it was too late, he needed to give God a helping hand and so he had intercourse with a maidservant Hagar who bore him a son named Ishmael. This was not the child of the promise and it wasn't until Abraham was ninety-nine that God intervened and Isaac was born. As the years went by Isaac became more and more precious to Abraham. In fact since his future was so tied up in his son, it is not unreasonable to presume that his identity became synonymous with Isaac. Then God did the unthinkable; he asked him to sacrifice his son. Abraham responded to the point of binding Isaac to the altar and holding a knife over him. Then an angel intervened and he was told not to lay a hand on the boy (Genesis 22:12). As a result of his obedience Abraham's descendants would become 'as many as the stars of Heaven and as countless as the grains of sand on the sea shore'. In being prepared to sacrifice Isaac his son, Abraham was also ready to relinquish his identity as Father. Precisely because of this he was eminently ready to become the Father of a multitude and ultimately our 'Father in Faith'.

The Father Wound

A large number of people find themselves quite uncomfortable with the concept of God as Father and are much more at home praying to Jesus. The Abba of the New Testament doesn't convey for them a sense of warmth and closeness but instead feels surprisingly cold and distant. A likely explanation for this is that if we could reach into a child's mind to determine how they see God we would probably be looking at the image of the child's own father. How we later relate to God as Father can be largely determined by how we saw, or didn't see, our physical father.

The father can be absent from the child's life in so many ways other than physically as in death or separation:

Being emotionally undemonstrative, distant or unavailable.
Unconsciously resenting the child for getting the attention he was denied at that age.
Abdicated his responsibility in favour of work or leisure.
Having his own unresolved childhood issues.
Alcoholism, drug abuse or pornographic addiction.
Having a too rigid or too relaxed discipline structure.
Mental, physical or emotional punishment, violence or sexual abuse.
Being unaware that he is using the child to fill his own emotional needs.

An important aspect of the father role for the boy growing up is to free him from his mother attachment and introduce him into the world of manhood. Where this doesn't take place, the male may present a macho image precisely because he is unsure of his masculinity. Or he may become effeminate and have a bi-sexual or homo-sexual orientation. Emotionally he is not free, his feminine side is too much in control and he may well marry a woman that he can call 'mum' and eventually treat her as such! In practice this means that he is likely to re-enact his early years, taking his partner for granted just as he would his mother. He may find responsibility very hard to take and he will be drawn towards living the life of single man similar to when he was a young adult.

For the daughter, part of the father role is to affirm her emerging femininity. In his masculinity her femininity can feel at home. Where this is absent she is likely to feel unsure of herself as a woman and either be drawn towards same sex relationships or spend much of her life searching for the father she didn't have in the various men she attracts into her life. Each of these relationships she will idealize but eventually cripple by a burden of unrealistic expectations. From her gaping father wound will come an inordinate need to be hugged, caressed and affirmed. Often this will cause her to trade sex for affection, but because this is operating at the unconscious level of the father-daughter relationship she usually senses something wrong, and may even speak the truth, that it feels 'incestuous'.

Ultimately, seeking the answer outside of oneself in someone else will not heal the father wound. Only by becoming father to that part of the hurting self can healing and resolution take place. This is when the relationship to God as Abba Father begins to become real.

4

The Inner Child

Parenting Our Lost Self

The Inner Child

The piece shaped like a small mushroom inside a larger one is entitled 'The Inner Child'. The wood used in both the outer and the inner mushroom is yew and comes from the same tree. No stain has been used on either piece and both are shown in their natural colours. The difference is that with the smaller, a foreign object at some stage was inserted into its material and has traumatized the wood. This may have been a nail or a constricting piece of wire tied around the branch many years earlier. This posed a threat to its very survival. Over time the surrounding wood, in its struggle to outgrow this obstacle, has undergone a cellular transformation that has resulted in a radical change of appearance. As such it is a powerful visual representation of the wounded and traumatized part of ourselves that has always been part of us, yet needs to be embraced by the adult.

It goes without saying that every adult was once a child. Each person's childhood takes place both within time and outside of time. The influences and events of our childhood, be they good or bad, are not left behind; rather they accompany us into adulthood and have enormous influence on our adult experience. While driving a car it is possible to check in the mirror for traffic coming from behind. Then on seeing nothing you pull out only to be alarmed at a vehicle, hooting its horn in annoyance, having appeared apparently out of nowhere. A 'blind spot' in the mirror has almost been our undoing. One of the most notorious blind spots on the psychological plane is our Inner Child. Even when we are in a regressive free-fall back to being a frightened toddler or a confused teenager, we are often totally blind to the reality of what is happening. In fact we usually find a thousand other reasons for feeling as terrible as we do and these can lead us down many cul-de-sacs in search of answers. When that part of ourselves that has been split off is trying to reconnect it appears to reverse the common message given to children, that 'they should be seen and not heard'. The inner child will indeed make itself heard but unfortunately also hides its face so we don't easily recognize when it is asking for our attention.

Who/What is the Inner Child?

The Child within is that part of us which is alive, creative, energetic and fulfilled. It is an essential part of who we really are as our real Self. In her beautiful book *The Drama of the Gifted Child* Alice Miller says, 'Only when I make room for the voice of the child within me do I feel myself to be genuine and creative'. The Prophet Isaiah, in Chapter 11, presents a wonderful picture of how the opposites within us, represented as traditional enemies, can be reconciled when the inner child is given its proper place. 'The wolf shall lie down with the lamb and the leopard shall lie down with the kid, the calf and the young lion shall browse together, with a little child to guide them'.

In the Gospel (Matthew 19: 13-15) there is a telling incident where Jesus is busy with ministry and people are bringing children to him. The reaction of the apostles was to try and stop them with the excuse that he was too busy. Jesus effectively scolds them saying, 'Let the children come to me for it is to such as these that the kingdom belongs.' From a psychological perspective the adult is often far too busy to listen to the needs of the inner child, yet wholeness is never possible without the child being given recognition. In another place Jesus says, 'Unless you change and become like little children you, cannot enter the Kingdom' (Matthew 10: 15). To become like little children is not to be childish, but rather to recognize and live from the child within which is part of our true selves.

Fig. 1 **Yew Egg** Fig. 2 **Egg Cups**

The Egg in fig. 1 is made from yew. It is a symbol of new life, potential and creativity. Fig.2 is a picture of the same egg that has been opened and transformed into two egg cups. Both pictures can represent the Inner Child part of us that is laden with potential and full of hidden possibilities.

The child who grows up in a dysfunctional home where parental conditions are not suitable is destined to become stifled and wounded. Such conditions might include:

- Alcoholism or Drug Abuse.
- Chronic Mental Illness.
- Serious Physical Illness.
- Unresolved Grief.
- Violence, Bitterness and Conflict.
- Neglect, Lack of mental stimulation.
- Rigidity, Control and Perfectionism.
- Lack of Discipline.
- Punishment as opposed to Discipline.
- Being compared with other siblings.
- Conditional Love.
- Child Abuse – Physical, Emotional, Mental, Sexual or Religious.

Such conditions may also be multi-generational which means that the problems didn't start with mother and father. Alcoholism, unresolved grief and abuse, are just some of the legacies that pass from one generation to another.

While the above list is large it is by no means exhaustive, leading researchers in this field suggest that somewhere between 80% and 95% of families fall into the dysfunctional category. If this is the case then an alarming number of children do not receive the love, guidance and nurturing necessary for them to form healthy relationships and enjoy feelings of high self-esteem and happiness.

Some words that characterize the plight of the Inner Child are:

ANXIETY /FEAR

HELPLESNESS

ABANDONMENT

CONFUSION

EMPTINESS

LONELINESS

UNHAPPINESS

LOSTNESS

The Long Journey Home

Growing up in a dysfunctional family system, the true Self goes into hiding and we try to become what we think others want us to be. This is the false or co-dependent self which takes over and runs our lives. The result is that we live our lives like victims where there is no stability in our relationships, and we keep repeating the same old patterns and experience life as a series of recycled traumas. This was what Freud called 'repetition compulsion'. Relying on the false self, we try to fill our emptiness with all kinds of people, places, and experiences from outside ourselves. We substitute outer journeys for inner ones. Carl Jung said of travel that at its best it is an expression of one's inner journey, but at its worst, is a substitute for it. It can take a long time to realize that, 'The eye is not filled with seeing or the ear with hearing', to borrow a phrase from the Book of Ecclesiastes. The accumulation of external materials and experiences ultimately fails to meet the inner emptiness precisely because the absence of things from the outside didn't cause the emptiness in the first place. What did cause it was that the child within went into hiding. Our true Self was lost, and with it the ability to connect with God, Life and others in a meaningful way.

Seeking The Lost

Luke, Chapter 15, contains the famous three parables of forgiveness and divine mercy. These are the story of the Lost Sheep, the Lost Coin and the Lost Son. Viewed psychologically the Prodigal Son story can be interpreted as our need to embrace the shadow side of our personality and this is dealt with in another chapter. However the first two are particularly relevant to our understanding the Inner Child. A shepherd has a hundred sheep and loses one, so he leaves the ninety-nine in the wilderness and goes in search of the lost. When he eventually tracks it down, he places it on his shoulders and returns home in jubilation. There is the implication that the ninety-nine are not complete without the one, just as the adult is not whole or complete without the inner child. Also the adult experience of life, of the ninety-nine, can be a wilderness until the search is successful.

There are varying degrees of feeling lost, depending on when the inner child was traumatized. In the Lost Sheep story the animal can at least cry out in its distress, whereas in the parable of the Lost Coin, the object is mute, there are no words. If the child part of us is wounded after the verbal stage of our development, there is the likelihood of its cry being expressed in some form of verbal manner. On the other hand if the damage was done prior to being able to speak, there will be no verbal expression but just raw, painful emotions. A child who has been rejected in the womb, or who has absorbed its mother's sadness while in the womb, will be totally at a loss for words to express how they feel. Similarly a child who was separated from its mother at birth, as in adoption, or where the mother was emotionally unavailable, will be at a similar loss for words and may express their reality in terms of being like an astronaut, cut adrift from the spaceship in outer space, with no centre of gravity.

Changing our perceptions

Children by virtue of their nature and age are wonderful receivers but hopeless interpreters. They pick up and absorb the emotional reality of everything that is going on, but do not have the mental capacity to understand the reasons behind what is taking place. A child may be traumatized by a long stay in hospital and have no comprehension that this was necessary in order to save its life. In order to fully parent ourselves it is necessary to uncover the core material of our early feelings, beliefs and memories. Most of this is illogical and emotionally very primitive. Yet all of this core material acts like a mental filter through which all our new experiences must pass.

(1 Event
(2 Evaluation
(3 Emotion

Using the three key words event, evaluation and emotion, it is not possible to move from number one to number three without passing through number two. The external event may be quite positive, as in one person showing affection to another. Yet because the core evaluation memory is one of abuse and betrayal, the final emotional reaction is likely to be one of suspicion and of feeling used. It is always this core material that shapes our experience. It is as if we were wearing sunglasses; no matter how strong the sunlight, it will always be filtered in the same manner. In order for our perceptions to be filtered in a new way we need a new set of visors. The core material has to be changed, and we can only hope to do this by making contact with and befriending the Inner Child.

In an earlier chapter we explored the significance of self-acceptance. There is no aspect of acceptance more important than learning to embrace our inner child. It is this part of us that holds the key to healthy relationships, to intimacy, physical energy, well-being, enthusiasm and creativity. Our Inner Child is the source of humour, fun and rejuvenation. When it is allowed to be itself and dwell in our heart it can lead us to a wellspring of great joy and wisdom.

The often long and painful journey to rediscover and parent our Inner Child finds appropriate expression in these lines from T. S. Eliot in his poem 'The Four Quartets'.

> *'We shall not cease from exploration,*
> *And the end of all our exploring*
> *Will be to arrive back where we started*
> *And know the place for the first time.'*

A Parenting Story

Catherine was five months pregnant and in her late thirties. A friend supported her into a counselling room suffering from complete nervous exhaustion. She helped her onto a couch and placed a blanket over her. Her two earlier pregnancies had been very difficult and characterized by months of sickness. In this case her vomiting had been so severe and prolonged that she required hospitalization. While there, her physical condition got a little better but her psychological state degenerated dramatically as she developed a hospital phobia. After being released she felt she was having a serious mental breakdown and was close to dying. As a child, from four to nine, Catherine was a victim of serious sexual abuse by a relative. At the age of seven both herself and her three-year-old sister were in hospital at the same time and placed in adjoining cots. She was deeply traumatized at seeing the little sister, whom she adored, being seriously beaten for crying. Her hospital phobia made perfect sense in the light of this.

Catherine spoke of her feelings and reactions now being those of a small child. She felt totally disconnected from herself and unable to relate to the adult world. It was as if she was a small six or seven-year-old terrified child again. As she had grown older, Catherine tried to get on with her life and put the past behind her. In fact she had left a large part of herself behind and now that the circumstances were right the past was coming back apparently to haunt her but, in reality, more to seek reintegration. The particular combination of events, being pregnant, preparing to give birth, and being in hospital, was the perfect combination to trigger the emergence of her Wounded Child. The disowned, rejected and traumatized part of herself was now crying out for her attention with such alarming intensity that it was even posing a real threat to her life.

When the light of awareness began to dawn as to what was really happening in her life, a remarkable transformation began to take place. Her eyes brightened and for the first time she began to move. She perked up, folded away the blanket and then sat up, She could feel her wounded little girl crying out to be held and loved. Knowing that her cry had gone unheeded for so many years she first apologized to that part of herself for her neglect and then created a special space in her heart into which she welcomed that child. Next she made a solemn commitment that she would always be there for that child. She promised that she would provide all that was needed for her to grow and become part of her adult Self. After just one hour of watching this amazing reunion, it was like seeing someone rise from the dead.

In the absence of such a vital connection being made with her Inner Child, the next step would have been referral for psychiatric care and medication. This would have made it even more difficult to discern what was going on. That kind of result was almost too alarming to contemplate. She would likely have given birth to a child that she could never connect with, and a baby would have been born who would never know its mother. The legacy of unfinished business would already be passed down to another generation, with the probability of surviving for many more. Four months later, Catherine had made a full recovery and gave birth to a lovely baby girl. Contrary to medical expectations she never experienced post-natal depression and continues to live a very normal and happy life.

5

The Masks We Wear.

Becoming Real

Yew Log

Before the inner beauty of any piece of wood can be revealed it is first necessary to strip away the bark. At the psychological level this corresponds to the persona or mask we wear. In the words of the poet T. S. Eliot it is, 'The face we put on to meet the faces that we meet.' Why do we hide our true Self and choose instead to live behind a mask? The answer can usually be traced back to childhood. Most people grow up in homes where there are varying degrees of dysfunctionality. Indeed we can consider ourselves lucky if we had parents who were, to use a phrase of Winnicott, simply 'good enough'. Even in homes where there was an abundance of love, there may have been a shortage of affection. Unconditional love, which is the basic need of every child, is a very scarce commodity. Where this is not forthcoming, the child begins to settle for attention and adopts a manner of behaving that reflects what he or she thinks others want him to be.

The mistaken belief is that by fulfilling others expectations they will get what they need. This doesn't happen and it is entirely possible to spend an entire lifetime trying to obtain from others what I failed to receive as a child. Usually with a strong persona there is an underlying sense of failure and an unspoken resentment that I am loved not for who I am, but for what I do. As a child, if I received recognition for being good and getting high grades, then my persona can take the form of always needing to appear good and successful. The downside is that we cannot always be good and we do have to cope with failure, and for the one living behind such a mask any falling short of their self imposed ideal is experienced as total failure. Usually when we identify our particular persona we find that it was our way of gaining recognition or of coping as a child. The one who is the joker and acts the clown may be covering up a lifetime of hurt and find himself trapped in the image of always having to be the life and soul of the party.

For others where there may have been a strong work ethic in the family, being the hard worker and the one who was capable of doing more than everyone else is adopted as the 'modus operandi persona.' Often this forms the base for workaholism where personal needs always take second place and can be easily sacrificed on the altar of work. Similarly the person who always has to please, and has difficulty saying 'no' and respecting their own boundaries, probably survived as a child by always going out of their way to be 'nice' and pleasing to everyone.

Shyness is a persona and for so many an affliction. For the more introverted personality type it is far easier to withdraw into oneself than to invest in any outward quest for approval. Shyness and fear tend to inhabit the same space and the challenge for such a person is to overcome their fears and allow that inner light which often shines brightly to be of service to others. While the tendency for those with an external persona is to overplay themselves in order to impress, the shy individual will tend to underplay their role. Here the words quoted by Nelson Mandela at his inaugural speech as President of South Africa are particularly appropriate: 'Playing small does not serve the world.' For most of us, the persona is something behind which we hide our real selves, and what we appear to be on the outside is not who we really are on the inside. The goal of psychological growth is that both should be as one, where what you see is what you get. It is who I am.

Before the deeper Self can emerge, the facade of the persona has to crumble. This can be a terrifying experience and is often experienced as a breakdown. Properly understood it is in fact a breakthrough where so much of what has been denied and repressed for so long is beginning to make an appearance. One of the most common ways in which dreams express this reality is in terms of nakedness. A woman in her forties who was slowly reclaiming her own identity after twenty years of being 'mother' had a recurring dream where she found herself on the public road close to her mother's house, but she was naked from the waist up.

Finally it must be acknowledged that it is also possible, and sometimes even necessary, to have a good and healthy persona. This is where the person is not hiding behind their mask, nor are they identified with it. A law enforcement officer is expected by the public to wear the policeman persona while he is on duty. If however he continues to be the policeman when he is at home and off duty, then that persona becomes an obstacle to him having a fatherly relationship with his kids and being truly intimate with his wife. To be the policeman, doctor, nurse or teacher is necessary but to have the freedom to be oneself is more important.

Envy – A Betrayal of Self

To envy someone is to compare myself with another and to see something in them, or see them as having something that I would like to have for myself. It is not to be confused with jealousy which is a form of possessiveness where I fear losing what I regard as mine. The root meaning of the word envy comes from the Latin 'invidere' which basically means to 'begrudge'. One of the inherent dangers of becoming too identified with a persona is that the true Self with all its richness, mystery and wonder is so hidden that we can only see it mirrored in others. Psychotherapy recognizes that envy is often the underlying cause of so many problems and rifts in human relationships. It is such a destructive emotion that

Christian tradition ranks it among the seven deadly sins. It is quite deadly in so far as it kills off Self–awareness and sees all that is missing outside in someone else rather than within oneself. The underlying message of envy, which may take many years to decode, is that it is a hunger for wholeness that has been thwarted. Envy is a particularly difficult emotion to recognize, and many go through their whole life always comparing themselves unfavourably with others.

The following are some of the tell-tale signs that this 'green eyed monster' is lurking in the shadows.

Idealization: This is a most common way of lessening our envious feelings. We put the other person on a pedestal and we love and admire them for being all that we are not. Usually when they don't live up to our expectations our love turns quickly to contempt.

Indecision: This can take the form of confusion and unclear thinking about big issues, such as getting married or career choice, down to the little things like what to eat or wear. The lack of ever having made a fundamental affirmation of Self makes all decisions difficult. The result is procrastination and indecision. A procrastinator has been described as someone who suffers from a hardening of the 'oughteries'. Shoulds, oughts and musts are often characteristics of the envious person.

Greed: This is really a neurotic inability to ever feel satisfied. The envious person easily falls prey to the myth of materialism that 'to have more, means to be more'. The word 'enough' seldom forms part of their vocabulary. The more they have the more they want. Like people forced to drink salt water to quench their thirst, the more they drink the thirstier they become.

Destructive Criticism: Probably the most common expressions of envy are backbiting and malicious gossip where other people are continually being 'cut down to size'. Talking disparagingly about someone else is very characteristic of envy. The good fortune of one person spells unhappiness for the one who is envious. This makes them secretly take pleasure in other people's misfortunes.

Excessive Independence: This often expresses itself in an inability to ask for help and having difficulty receiving. To do so would be to acknowledge the strength of someone else which the envious one wants to avoid at all costs.

Ultimately envy gives more pain to the envier than to the envied. To quote from a Jewish writer of the eighteenth century:

'Envy is nothing but want of reason and foolishness, for the one who envies gains nothing for himself and deprives the one he envies of nothing. He only loses thereby… There are those who are so foolish that if they perceive their neighbour to possess a certain good, they brood and worry and suffer to the point that the neighbour's good prevents them from enjoying their own.'

Envy is every bit as common as love or anger and just as powerful. However, because we are slow to admit something so demeaning, it becomes part of our shadow and so can exercise enormous influence in our lives. Whether we are consumed by envy, or just afflicted with this unwelcome visitor from time to time, it is so important that we acknowledge, recognize it for what it is, decode its meaning, and claim our wholeness.

6

Featuring Defects

The Stone Rejected

Yew Vase

A Feature is an Accepted Defect

The vase shown is made from yew and has an unusual elongated heart shaped feature. This makes it both more interesting and more valuable. While rough turning the original wood, which on the surface looked in quite good condition, the rotting part soon became obvious. Seeing the extent of the defect the first impulse was to discard the piece as firewood. The next was to accept the defect as it was, treat it with extra care, and incorporate it into the overall design. The result of embracing the defect meant that the overall piece was saved and the defect was transformed into a valuable feature.

In Shakespearean Tragedy the principal character, like Hamlet, Macbeth or King Lear is portrayed as having a 'tragic flaw' in their make up. As the drama unfolds this 'flaw' inevitably brings about their ultimate downfall and destruction. Just how easy it is to allow one apparently negative aspect life to spoil the whole picture is encountered in many different ways, both in personal experience, and in the practice of psychotherapy.

Rachel, an attractive sixteen year old, sat crying her heart out and said, 'I just want to die, I hate myself so much'. On two occasions already she had attempted to take an overdose. Part of me sat wondering what on earth could be so seriously troubling this beautiful girl? She should have had the world as her oyster, yet she wants to end it all. 'What is it about yourself that you hate so much', I gently asked? She immediately replied, 'My front teeth are so ugly'. For the first time I noticed that her teeth were indeed somewhat out of shape, but not to any huge extent and this made me very curious to hear her story regarding her teeth. Up to the age of nine she was hardly even aware that she had teeth except when she got the odd toothache. Her pretty features were the envy of some girls in her class who began to ridicule her by making fun of her teeth. With development into puberty, her self-consciousness became increasingly overshadowed by teeth consciousness, to the extent that when she thought of herself she could only think of her teeth. Similarly she was convinced that when in contact with others all they could see were her crooked teeth. In rejecting this one aspect of herself she had come perilously close to destroying every other aspect of herself as well.

In such cases it is as if a mental filter has been in operation serving to exclude the positive and focus entirely on the negative. Another useful analogy is that of putting a drop of ink into a glass filled with water and the entire picture becomes clouded. In most cases of people contemplating taking their own lives it becomes clear that they are not so much wanting to kill themselves, as wanting to kill off something about themselves that they don't like. They don't really want to die, but there is something they can't live with. When this does happen, the potential for the flaw or defect to become a feature is destroyed and it is indeed tragic.

The Gospel Story of the Man with the Withered Hand (Luke 6:6) provides some useful insights into the healing of this common scenario. Going into the synagogue Jesus sees a man whose hand is withered. The hand is the instrument of touch and something he needed for employment. Not only had it limited his ability to be productive, but most likely it has made him the butt of jokes and ridicule as he grew up. It is not unreasonable to presume therefore that it was not just his hand that was withered, but also it represented his whole life. As the first part of his healing Jesus calls him to stand out in front. People like him generally prefer to stay in the background. Coming forward required courage and acceptance of his worth as a person. Next Jesus asked him to stretch out his hand. On the surface this seems a simple straightforward request, yet at a deeper level it had the power to challenge him to the core. His hand was what he was most ashamed of, and what he most wanted to keep hidden. Now he's being asked to expose it in full view of everybody. Then in that moment of acceptance, the miracle of wholeness took place.

In Mark 12:10, Christ is described as, 'The stone rejected by the builders, that has become the key stone.' This we are told is God's doing and it is marvellous to behold. The part of ourselves that we are most likely to reject is also that which, once accepted, has the greatest potential to help us define clearly who we really are, and so the overall transformation is indeed both marvellous and miraculous.

There is a growing trend in Japanese culture that also highlights the value of imperfection. This is the cult of *'Wabi Sabi*, which is the celebration of that which is flawed. People seek collectibles and attribute value to them simply on the basis that the item is cracked or flawed in some manner. The perfect item is not valued or considered whole on the basis that it is simply too perfect.

A few lines from one of Leonard Coen's songs captures the wisdom of seeking after wholeness rather than impossible ideal of perfection:

'Leave aside your perfect offering, there's a crack in everything, that's where the light gets in'.

Not *what* we see but *how* we see!

Duck or Rabbit?

The piece shown can be viewed in two entirely different ways. From one perspective it is seen as a rabbit while from another it is a duck. The same reality is totally changed by our perception. It is not always 'what' we see in life that makes us happy, miserable or sick, but 'how' we see it. A stumbling block can also be viewed as a stepping-stone while a setback can also become a springboard. One of our most limiting beliefs is that our past is real and permanent, that history cannot be changed. Yet we can continually re-write and re-create our past by changing our perceptions. A great Russian writer once said that two things can awaken the human spirit, they say that love can but suffering will.' This is found to be true when we can look back on a particularly turbulent episode or traumatic event, and realize how much we have matured and learned, and how it has made us what we are. Then we are seeing it in a very different light and it has lost all its power to influence our lives in a negative manner. The genesis of a particularly fruitful vocation is often found in the most unlikely and unwholesome places and experiences. Many of the best counsellors and psychotherapists find themselves specializing in areas where they themselves were most deeply hurt. Having resolved their own issues, they are now best qualified to lead others through theirs.

A Past Revisited

The Moses of the Exodus story is an excellent example of a past revisited and redeemed. At the age of forty he was described as 'a man mighty in word and deed'(Acts 7:22). Having grown up as a member of the royal household of Pharaoh he was the one person who could have been a voice for the voiceless multitude of his people who were in slavery in Egypt. Yet this opportunity was lost when he murdered an Egyptian who was ill-treating one of the Israelites. This caused him to flee to the land of Midian, a name that very appropriately means 'strife'. There he remained for another forty years before the next stage of his life dramatically unfolded. In Biblical terms the number forty signifies an end and a beginning. Moses had finally reached the end of his egotistical strength, his days of running were over, and he was ready to embrace his destiny. Chapter 3 of Exodus opens with Moses leading the flock of Jethro his father-in-law across the desert when God called to him from the burning bush. Many years of minding sheep in a harsh desert terrain was far beneath his dignity for a man of his calibre, yet it was an essential part of his training. Very soon he would be drawing on all that vast experience in leading the flock of his Heavenly Father across the same desert. In the divine economy even the apparently wasted years in the land of strife were an essential part of the overall plan.

Turning to the New Testament, we read of Christ growing to maturity and living the life of a humble carpenter in Nazareth. Not until the age of thirty does he leave his home and adopt the life of a wandering Rabbi. Research seems to indicate that Nazareth where he spent his hidden years was far from being a popular place to live and was probably at the bottom rung of the social ladder. This prompted the question, 'Can anything good come from Nazareth?' (John. 1:46). Yet it was from Nazareth that the Christ of ministry came forth as the long awaited Messiah. So it is often from our hidden suffering and 'Nazareth' years that the essential core of who we are and what our lives are about is being defined.

It is this final definition, which has the power to transform all our perceptions about what went before.

Perfectly Imperfect

Well Got At

Perfectly Whole

The piece shown is the reverse side of the piece on the opening page. It is entitled 'Well got at' for very obvious reasons. It is a unique piece of nature sculpture that carries an enormous history. It originated in the Amazon Rain Forest and was already over a hundred years old when Columbus set out on his voyage of discovery in 1492. Around 1800 it was cut down and became part of a ship that sank 20-30 years later. Because it is denser than water it lay on the seabed for almost two centuries. There it endured enormous onslaughts from its marine environment that fashioned its unique features. Eventually it was recovered and with a minimum of work was cleaned, varnished and given pride of place in my collection.

The symbolic significance of this piece was brought home to me in the context of a counselling session. A man in his late twenties described his life as, 'A total mess and almost beyond redemption.' He had been seriously abused as a child and many other horrible things had happened to him along the way, coupled with many shameful things he himself had done. After four sessions, he felt that while he had made some progress he now appeared to be stuck. Every now and then his gaze drifted towards the piece in the picture that stood in the corner of the room. He told me that it was like a magnet drawing him. I asked him why he was so fascinated by it. His reply took me somewhat by surprise: 'It's so perfectly imperfect, and yet it's perfectly whole.' The piece was acting as a mirror in which he could see himself. At an early age he had been 'got at', and all sorts of imperfections now marred his life. Yet the piece also held for him the image and possibility of wholeness. If he could only embrace his woundedness and face his truth, then his life could once again become a thing of beauty and worth. His identification with the piece was the crucial turning point in his life, and he went on from there to make a remarkable recovery.

7

Mistakes and Remakes

The Long and Winding Road

Redesigns in Yew

'There are no mistakes, just opportunities for redesign'.

The above is a well-known saying from the world of woodturning which every turner has found to be a useful guiding principle. The vases shown are my earliest examples of this principle in operation. During the work each piece took on a life of its own greatly helped by a momentary loss of concentration where a chisel slipped and the delicate wall was shattered. Instead of consigning the damage to the bin, I decided to redesign the piece, with a result that seemed more attractive than what I had originally intended.

In Jeremiah 18:1-6 there is a beautiful example of this principle in operation from the divine perspective. The prophet is told to go to the potter's house. There he sees the potter taking a shapeless mass of clay, plop it on the wheel, and attempt to make it into a graceful shape. When it doesn't turn out as he wishes, he doesn't discard the piece; instead he dampens it down, and begins to mould it into an entirely different object. Jeremiah was quick to understand the reassuring lesson. God isn't finished with us when things go wrong, when we become flawed by failure, or misshapen by events, He still wants to make something beautiful and useful out of our lives. The message of the potter is quite clear; the real sin in life is not to have made a mess of things, but rather to give up on ourselves because of that mess.

The Jericho Road

In Luke chapter 10, the story of the Good Samaritan, a man is on his way from Jerusalem to Jericho when he falls prey to robbers. For the Jews Jerusalem was their place of worship, it was the City of God, the place of Light and as the name suggests, the place of Peace. Jericho is the lowest city on earth, and for someone to be going from Jerusalem to Jericho meant symbolically that they had turned their back on the Light. They were heading in the wrong direction.

In human experience this is one of the more familiar and most travelled roads in life. It is the place where the concept of 'sin' easily finds a home in our understanding. We so easily find ourselves 'Jericho bound', robbed of our dignity and stripped of our self-esteem for many reasons. Usually it's as a consequence of the wrong choices we have made. However, it can just as easily be the result of how we have reacted to others when they have mistreated us and also how we have responded to some of life's more serious blows. Deciding to make the return journey from Jericho to Jerusalem is really about coming back to our true selves. In Christian teaching this is what we understand as 'repentance', which literally means to rethink, have a change of heart, or to turn around.

The Cul-de-Sac of Remorse

One of the pitfalls on the journey is to indulge in feelings of remorse, which the Monaghan poet Patrick Kavanagh aptly calls, 'The Devil's contrition'. This is the place of self-punishment where the guilt is held onto and the pride involved doesn't allow a process of self-forgiveness to begin. It is quite common for someone, who at a conscious level desires success and happiness, to continually undermine their best efforts because of an unconscious desire for self-punishment. A rather strange feature of holding onto guilt is that the bearer, in order to fulfill their need for self-punishment, often repeats the original wrongdoing or sinks to an even lower level. This in turn sets up a spiral effect that is extremely difficult to break. An extreme case of this is where someone commits a serious crime and the guilt factor is so great as to propel that individual to commit a similar action over and over again.

Remorse also takes the form of holding onto regrets and self-recrimination. 'If onlys', invariably imprison us in the past. They take from our quality of life in the present and rob us of hope for the future. Regrets are like a crown of thorns, which we place on our own heads, and only we have the power to remove them.

Taking Responsibility

Because a matter is understandable, that doesn't make it excusable!

Maturity has been defined as the ability to take responsibility for both the foreseen and the unforeseen consequences of our own actions. The opposite of taking responsibility is to apportion blame to someone else with the result that we see ourselves as helpless victims. In the Genesis Story when Adam is called to account by God for having eaten the fruit of the forbidden tree, he fails to take responsibility. He blames Eve and, by implication, God himself. 'It was the woman *you* put with me, she tempted me and I ate'. Next when Eve is confronted, she also reneges and replies 'It was the serpent'. The serpent needless to say hadn't a leg to stand on! This tendency, so innate in human nature, perhaps throws light on the difficult concept of Original Sin. When God gave Moses the Ten Commandments at Sinai, it has been suggested that he left an important one out: Thou shalt not blame. In the Exodus story it was because of their sin of blaming and complaining that the generation of Israelites who were delivered from Egypt all died in the wilderness and never reached the Promised Land. When we blame, we give away the very power we need to bring about change in our own lives. While it is always wise to seek understanding as to why we have acted in a particular manner, it should never be used as an excuse for apportioning blame. Maturity always demands taking responsibility. Taking responsibility is an essential ingredient for personal growth. The more responsibility we take, the more power we have to create our lives as we want them to be.

Some of the clues that I may be abdicating responsibility are the following:

Blaming someone else for what I am saying, doing, or how I am feeling.

Blaming myself, where I become a victim of myself.

Allowing someone else too much power to control and dominate my life.

Expecting someone else to make me happy.

Upset, anger and wanting vengeance.

Always being the victim and feeling 'hard done by'.

Using the phrase, 'After all I did for so and so and this is how they treat me'.

Repeating the same old patterns.

Judging, criticizing and griping.

Envy, helplessness and self-pity.

Trying to manipulate and control others.

Impatience and disappointment.

Feeling stuck in a forever state of Limbo.

Fatigue and joylessness.

Being too passive / Avoiding confrontation.

Lack of focus / Feeling scattered.

Being over sensitive and taking things personally.

Obsessions and Addictions.

Guilt and Shame

Laburnum Jug

The laburnum jug shown is another example of a design by accident! This resulted from a series of mistakes. Notice the face feature that was revealed in the process of redesign. Perhaps a self-portrait!

Although they are often confused, there is a significant difference between the two closely related emotions of guilt and shame. The former is the emotion we experience as a result of doing something we believe to be wrong. It makes us feel bad because it separates us from our true Selves and from others. In this way it can serve a positive function insofar as it can act as a deterrent preventing us from repeating a harmful act. Its purpose is not to punish but rather to help us learn from our mistakes. Because guilt always comes from the past, it keeps the past alive. It is a way to avoid the reality of the present. Guilt drags the past into the future: a past of guilt will create a future of guilt. Only by releasing our guilt through confession and self-forgiveness can we let go of the past and begin creating a new future.

Shame is another painful and troublesome emotion that goes much deeper and is far more destructive than guilt. If guilt affects the ego, then the target of shame is the true Self or the core of a person's identity. Shame can come from old guilt. The guilt that attacks our consciousness becomes the shame that assaults our soul. While guilt is about what I did, shame is about who I think I am. Guilt can be understood as, 'I made a mistake', whereas shame thinks, 'I am a mistake'. Usually both guilt and shame have their roots in childhood before we have any sense of our own identity. As children we were often told when we made a mistake, 'You should be ashamed of yourself'. Although it was usually spoken without malice, the statement had the potential to be most damaging. At a young age we are still unaware that we are not to be identified with our mistakes and while we may have done something wrong it is not we who are wrong. Many experiences such as being punished, abused, bullied or ridiculed can compound our sense of shame. Our feelings of hurt anger and resentment tend to get buried and we end up feeling bad about ourselves.

One feature of shame is that it makes us hide our faces, and not be able to look another straight in the eye. This is an indication of how our sense of Self has been wounded. The healing of this issue involves revisiting our shameful memories and reconnecting with these painful emotions. Acknowledgement of past issues paves the way for forgiveness which in turn allows us to let them go. Our true Selves deserve not just divine mercy but also our forgiveness in order to be set free from the burden of guilt and shame. As we complete the process, and take the steps that are necessary, our self-image is restored.

8

Befriending the Shadow

The Dark Side of Self

Bird of Paradise

The 'Bird of Paradise' piece, also used in a later chapter, provides a useful illustration of the difference between perfection and wholeness. The piece of bog oak is riddled with cracks and defects. To seek perfection would be to destroy the wood of its potential and reduce it almost entirely to chippings. However, by incorporating the imperfections the character of the piece has had the chance to emerge. A too narrow concept of perfection is unable to accommodate wholeness. Wholeness not only accommodates imperfection but also depends upon it for its very existence.

Writing in his work on dreams, Carl Jung said, 'There is no light without shadow and no psychic wholeness without imperfection. To round itself out, life calls not for perfection but for completeness; and for this the 'thorn in the flesh' is needed, the suffering of defects without which there is no progress and no ascent.'

When I reflect on my young days, the text from Scripture that I heard most often used as a base for sermons was the one from Matthew 5: 48, 'You must be perfect as the Heavenly Father is perfect'. Much of the spirituality of the time seemed to centre around an idea of 'perfection' which gave the impression that holiness allowed for no trace of shadow or impurity. Perfection was essentially about the elimination of all imperfections in one's life. Even at a young age, the idea of a person without any thoughts or emotions that could be regarded as in any way sinful or wrong seemed totally unrealistic and very unattractive.

During my Seminary days I was still intrigued by this seemingly impossible notion of 'perfection' and was delighted to have the opportunity to examine its exact meaning. The Greek sense of the word means 'being brought to an end state' or 'being brought to completion'. Understood in this light the passage is the Lord's invitation to become what we were created to become through the unfolding of our inner Self. Even the word 'Salvation', so common in Christian usage, confirms this, since it comes from the Latin 'salus' meaning 'health', it also implies wholeness. Completion or wholeness is far from being perfection in the narrow, one-sided meaning of the word that we were used to. Instead, it is a paradoxical wholeness; where a person's faults and failures are incorporated and transformed and even contribute to the achievement of one's greatest potential and capacity for love.

'Be You Perfect' ~~~~~ 'Be Perfectly You'!

This understanding of what perfection really means also makes the Kingdom of God a reality in each person's life, which is capable of being enjoyed in the here and now. It is precisely the process of inner growth into wholeness and creativity which constitutes the coming of the Kingdom into someone's life. Also by being part of our inner development the great creator God of the universe becomes as close to us as that same creative process.

Yin-Yang

The Yin-Yang Symbol provides a useful illustration of the interplay between light and darkness. The circle suggests wholeness, yet neither light nor darkness is capable of finding completion without the other.

There is in human nature a very real tendency to split off or separate ourselves from painful or shameful experiences. We lock the door on them in the mistaken belief that if ignored they will go away. The same is true for thoughts, feelings and urges that we do not want to acknowledge. We try to hide them, not just from others, out of fear of rejection, but also from ourselves, because they contradict the image of whom we want to be. What we deem unacceptable and repress into the cellar of our unconscious will always express itself in an even more unacceptable form. This is where the Lord's command to love the enemy takes on a whole new meaning. Normally we think of the enemy as someone outside ourselves, but the real enemy can be within. The more we have split off, or denied this inner enemy, the more shocked we are likely to be when it does sooner or later appear.

In their understanding of the Shadow, Freud and Jung differed considerably. For Freud the Shadow was like a repository or cellar where we buried the unacceptable aspects of ourselves. Jung on the other hand regarded it as 'pure gold'. In his view it was 'not just evil by nature, it is also the source of the highest good: not only dark but also light; not only bestial, semi-human and demonic, but superhuman, spiritual and in the classical sense of the word, Divine'.

Accepting the Seemingly Unacceptable

An essential part of the inner journey is to reclaim what has been lost in the Shadow. As expressed in the Yin-Yang symbol, we humans are a mixture of light and darkness, good and evil. We are capable of the highest levels of sanctity and the lowest levels of depravity. Becoming aware of our multidimensional selves, and integrating our Shadow side, is an ongoing process throughout life. It is never achieved once and for all, but requires a constant attitude of welcoming, recognizing, healing and harmonizing our inner life. This constitutes the essence of spirituality. If we equate holiness with perfection then we will never recognize the Shadow and it will take on a life of its own. If on the other hand it is given the attention it requires, then instead of being our worst enemy, it will become our most powerful ally.

Unmasking the Shadow of Inferiority

Countless people spend their entire life suffering from the crippling effects of an inferiority complex. They never fulfill their own potential and fear prevents them from giving of their best to others. A sense of inadequacy and low self-esteem makes them dependent and passive. Many feel they have little to offer and little to say. They rarely feel 'good enough' to make a creative contribution. Feeling cut off from the wellsprings of their own life they rely too much on others for a sense of happiness and well-being. Normally we project our unacceptable traits unto people, but inferiority arises as a result of projecting our positive aspects. Here it is our strengths, our underdeveloped gifts and talents that are being repressed and attributed to others. Such people we tend to put on pedestals where we overvalue their gifts, admire their achievements, and secretly resent not being like them. Projecting our positive shadow can be a real 'cop out' where we avoid the responsibility to develop and use our talents and abilities in the service of others.

Shadow Projections and Relationships

Refusal to face our shadow usually means that we project it onto others. We will see and judge in others what we are blind too in ourselves. Shadow projections are at work behind the scenes whenever we find ourselves involved in arguments and conflicts, when we need to control and have our own way, and especially when being right seems more important than being in relationship!

A woman who had numerous affairs and was a bad alcoholic for many years recovered from her addiction. In dissociating herself from her past she became intolerably self-righteous and moralistic with her daughters. The person she did not want to know she projected onto them. So great was that burden that two of the girls became what she despised, promiscuous and over-indulgent, replicas of her earlier self.

David was someone who was insanely jealous and possessive of his wife. He continually accused her of having affairs, and became violent when he saw her having the most innocent of interactions with other men. For a man to stop and speak to her on the street was enough to send him into a rage. On two occasions she ended up in hospital with a badly bruised body just for having danced with another man at a social gathering. In fact David himself had had a number of affairs, and the burden of his own infidelity, which he never acknowledged, was what he was projecting onto his wife.

Rosie was a woman who liked to give 'a holier than thou' impression and occupy the higher moral ground on all issues of morality. When her daughter became pregnant out of wedlock she gave the girl such a hard time that she suffered a nervous breakdown. The fact that this woman herself had also had a child before marriage and had it adopted only emerged several years later.

Projection of the Shadow is also the root cause of racism. Because the word black carries connotations of the darker side of our moral nature, which we hate and fear, it has throughout history been projected by whites onto blacks. All that the whites found unacceptable in themselves they projected onto the unfortunate blacks.

The holocaust of six million Jews during the Second World War can also be understood as a product of projection. The Nazis identified themselves as the superior Arian race. They were no longer able to recognize their own inferior qualities. The Jews then had to carry the burden of fear and self-loathing that the Nazis had for themselves. The concentration camps became the expression of the Nazi attempt to exterminate their own inner enemy. In so doing they joined the ranks of the most despised groups on the earth.

For centuries within the Catholic Church the area of sexuality was repressed, denied and denigrated. So great was the attempt to control this monstrous Shadow that many religious orders even resorted to whipping themselves whenever sexual thoughts or urges were the cause of temptation. Moral teaching became largely focused on this area, to the extent that bad thoughts became solely identified with sexual thoughts. The threat of mortal sin became the great deterrent to avoid any deviation from the 'straight and narrow', Yet it is precisely this area which has been the cause of so much scandal, ridicule and loss of respect for the Institutional Church in recent times. It has now become apparent, that even during the years when the sexual Shadow was considered to be most securely under lock and key, it was expressing itself in the most bizarre and repulsive form possible in the form of is in fact an urgent call to adopt a completely new outlook to this beautiful aspect of human nature.

An area where the Shadow is very easily recognized, especially in others, is in the arena of work. Personal needs for intimacy, family and leisure, are so often sacrificed on the altar of achievement. Here in particular we can see the words of Christ so often fulfilled: 'Someone gaining the world' in the sense of getting to the top, but at the expense of losing his or her soul in the process.

Ultimately it is not our Shadow that is evil, but rather our rejection or our denial of it. As long as we fail to give it acknowledgement it will cause us to suffer the most embarrassing contradictions and the gravest humiliations. Yet on the other hand if it is recognized and accepted it will reveal its positive side and compliment rather than contradict our lives.

The Stranger and the Estranged

In the Judaeo-Christian tradition there is a strong emphasis on welcoming the stranger. This is one of the most recurring motifs running throughout both the Old and the New Testament. Normally this has been interpreted in an external manner, as someone out there, but ultimately it is our relationship with the inner stranger or the part of ourselves from which we have become estranged, that will determine how we will treat the outer stranger. Should we lack the courage to face and be reconciled with every aspect of our total Self, we will be destined to encounter in a negative manner our disowned parts in others.

Depending on how we view it, the most famous parable in the world is of the Prodigal Son, and it also expresses the truth of the need to be reconciled with our Shadow. When the pleasure-loving spendthrift returns home after his years of debauchery, the father invites his eldest brother to join in the celebratory feast. This is the one who was always responsible, who always sought to please and be what the father wanted him to be. Yet he was self-righteous, unforgiving and joyless. Taken as two inner figures, they represent the two halves of the personality, and both need to come into a right relationship with each other before the celebration of wholeness is truly complete. If that happens the older one can give to the younger a sense of maturity and responsibility, while the younger will add humour, sparkle, joy, fun, and compassion to his elder brother. It is in this reconciliation of apparent opposites that the Kingdom of God is established.

'One of the best days of my life was when I decided to rebaptise all my negative qualities as my best qualities.' Nietzsche.

In his beautiful book *Anam Chara*, John O'Donohue, with whom I shared my seminary days, has a beautiful piece that expresses the essence of what has been written above, He writes:

'Our lives would be immeasurably enriched if we could but bring the same hospitality to meet the negative as we bring to the joyful and the pleasurable. In avoiding the negative we only encourage it to recur. We need a new way of understanding and integrating the negative. The negative is one of the closest friends of our destiny. It contains essential energies, which we need and cannot find elsewhere.

When we notice something immoral, we normally tend to be harsh with ourselves and employ moral surgery to remove it. In doing this we are only ensuring that it remains trapped within. We merely confirm our negative view of ourselves and ignore our potential for growth. There is a strange paradox in the soul that if we try to avoid or remove the awkward quality it will pursue you. In fact the only way to still its unease is to transfigure it, let it become something creative and positive that contributes to who you are.

When you decide to practice inner hospitality, your self-torment ceases. The abandoned, neglected and negative selves come into a seamless unity.'

9

Mirror Image

As Within so Without

God and life have so many ways of teaching us what we most need to know but often least want to hear about ourselves. Having the courage to look at what is happening in our lives, especially if it keeps on recurring, can provide us with a lot of insight and material for reflection and personal growth. Unfortunately, we tend to be so programmed into seeing ordinary everyday events as random and meaningless, that when truth comes knocking on our door we may seldom recognize it. The outer reality can act as a very useful reflection of our inner lives and many situations can provide opportunities for us to learn and to grow.

Carl Jung made the observation that what we don't face up to and deal with in our lives will keep on recurring as 'fate'. The more unaware we are of unresolved issues, the greater the influence they will exert over us. Having the courage to acknowledge recurring patterns allows us to make conscious choices and diminishes the effect they can have in our lives.

Pic. 1 **Natural Edge Yew Bowl**

Pic. 2 **Mirror Image**

Pic. 1 is of a natural edged yew bowl and Pic. 2 is of the same bowl showing two star shaped cracks almost identical on each side and mirroring one another. It provides a useful visual image of the truth 'as within, so without'. Like the bowl, nobody is perfect, but what is perfect are the situations we create in order to learn the lessons we need to grow. Wisdom comes from the willingness to learn from every situation and to see each one as a gift, a chance to learn something important about ourselves.

Mark lost his job on three successive occasions because he verbally abused his employer when being corrected over a piece of work. Fate was shouting at his door and on opening it he saw his father in the mists of memory shouting abuse at him for not measuring up. Carrying such an unresolved, destructive legacy from childhood made him unable to hear constructive criticism as an adult and consequently this was a major block to his personal growth and development.

Patricia described her experience of life as one of continually getting 'stuck'. Feeling 'stuck' was almost her badge of identity. Getting stuck in traffic jams, stuck in airports, stuck in lifts, feeling stuck in jobs, in unsuitable accommodation, and in numerous relationships. The outer reality was reflecting the inner reality of a three-year-old that had fallen into a shallow, disused well and being stuck in the mud for a terrifying period of time before her cries were heard. Revisiting the memory, both verbally and emotionally, brought her into wonderful freedom and released the hold that fate held over her life.

Mirroring Relationships

When we make choices about those we wish to be in close relationship with, there is an underlying principle involved that is not usually recognized, but yet powerfully at work. 'Birds of a feather stick together', is an old saying that expresses something of this truth. We generally assume that our choice of partner is based on what is right or good for us. In fact our own stage of maturity, mentally, emotionally and spiritually, is a determining factor in all relationships. In essence this means that I choose relationships with those who are more or less at the same place as myself in terms of the overall maturation process and I will tend to avoid those who are at a different stage of development. At one level, opposites attract, but at a deeper dimension, like also attracts like.

This is a principle of selection that has some far reaching implications:

Emotional maturity is an essential prerequisite for genuine intimacy.

Changing partners without changing oneself can make little difference.

The kind of person I am drawn towards reveals so much about myself.

While in a therapeutic process the search for intimacy with another may not be wise.

Personal change and growth will seriously challenge established relationships.

The more mature a person becomes the more they will reject co-dependency.

Inner growth and development may be resented by those who are not prepared to change.

Becoming whole may involve separation or rejection and can be a solitary journey.

Inner Reality affecting Outer Reality

Sometimes we know what we want, or at least we think that we know. The achievement of our goal seems straightforward enough yet we can mess it up and sabotage our chances. Then we get annoyed with ourselves. At some level we sense that it is our inner reality that is creating our outer reality, so something of our deeper Self needs attention. Perhaps the big reason that we don't always achieve our goals is that we are here to learn how to create our own reality and in the process to get to know a lot more about ourselves. I may long for success in my chosen career; I may be bright, creative, hardworking and have all the right qualifications and, yet something prevents it from coming about. Perhaps my deepest belief is that success always comes at too high a price and I need to look at how that is preventing me from taking necessary risks. I may consciously desire happiness but another unconscious factor comes into play that doesn't allow it to happen. Could it be that at the deeper level I still want to punish myself?

Where my unconscious mind is at variance with my conscious attitude, the unconscious will always win out.

A good example of how the unconscious exercises control was with Aisling, an attractive professional woman in her late thirties who seemed to be caught in a cycle of self-defeat. As soon as she would reach the point in her career where her success was gaining recognition, she would resign and take up a position with another firm. Her decisions were not made on the basis of climbing the professional ladder but were backward moves that sabotaged her career and left her starting almost from scratch. She was a very talented and gifted young woman who quickly moved up the ranks in her work. But, why was it that every time she became successful she would stab herself in the foot by handing in her notice? This was the mystery that prompted her to seek help in order to uncover her unconscious motivation.

What emerged was that as a child she had felt unwanted and had often been told so by her mother, who was herself a very unhappy woman. This had the effect of making Aisling feel that she was responsible for her mother's feelings and with it came the belief that she wasn't important and that she didn't matter. This truth became so ingrained in her memory that it dictated how she saw herself, the choices she made, and the direction she gave to her life. It followed that to do well for herself in her career was both wrong and selfish. She did not deserve to achieve success and to be happy. This was the unconscious belief at the core of her irrational behaviour that was denying her so much satisfaction and enjoyment. This new-found awareness enabled her to let go of those old, limiting beliefs and make some very positive choices in regard to her life and career. The result was that within three years she became one of the most respected professionals in her field.

Andrew was a man in his late thirties who suffered from stress and anxiety. He was extremely hardworking, conscientious, committed and reliable. Because of all these noble qualities, in the three firms he had worked with, he had received quick promotion and the burden of responsibility always fell on his shoulders. He now found himself collapsing under the strain. On the other two occasions he had simply quit his job, but this time he asked himself what was this saying to him, and wondering if there was something that he needed to learn. He was the eldest in his family with two younger sisters. His father had died suddenly when he was twelve and he tried to take responsibility for being the 'man of the house' from there on. As a teenager he was burdened with responsibility far beyond his years and felt a sense of failure at not being able to fill his father's shoes. Now as an adult he was the ideal person to be in a management position, but until he looked after the teenager part of himself, responsibility would always awaken the old ghost of failure and cause him stress and anxiety.

A Timely Reminder

Time Extension

Living in a fishing village and with a strong affinity to the sea I enjoy having a little motor-boat which, in the summer of 1997, developed some serious engine problems. All the parts were available except for one. This was part of the oil pump system. After two frustrating months of fine weather waiting on dry land for this part to arrive, I was told that it was not available and had yet to be manufactured. Then one day a neighbour who knew my problem put a question to me, one that I had on several occasions posed to her, 'What do you think that is saying to you*?*'

I reasoned that at a symbolic level the pump could represent the heart, so I resolved to have a cholesterol check. Within minutes of my decision the phone rang to say that the part had been located and was in the post. This confirmed that something significant was happening. I then went to the doctor for the test to discover that my cholesterol was at a dangerously high level and that I required urgent medication. The old part of the engine I held onto and in due time mounted on a piece of wood. Setting a clock on top seemed a very appropriate symbolic gesture since I felt it had given me more time!

10

Forgiven and Forgiving

The Road to Freedom

The Crossroads of Forgiveness

Forgiveness is represented as a crossroads with the centre pillar as the present, and the other two signposts as past and future. It is significant that the sign representing the past is made mostly from the darker wood and points downwards. Forgiveness can be understood as a moment in the present, which releases us from darkness of the past and opens up a bright new future.

Guilt and Resentment

Two issues basic to the human condition are guilt and resentment. As human beings we need to be forgiven and to forgive. The feeling of guilt may have arisen from violating a spiritual principle, but its purpose is not to punish us; it is to deter us from repeating that harmful act. Holding onto guilt is a way of clinging to the past. It paralyses effectiveness in the present, and it also provides a wonderful excuse to avoid taking responsibility for life here and now. Guilt destroys my capacity for happiness. By reminding us of the terrible wrongs we have done, and how we deserve to be punished, it makes us feel unworthy of having any happiness or good fortune in our lives. Much guilt is experienced not from deliberate wrongdoing, but as a consequence of not loving ourselves. With a negative self-image any form of self-indulgence can become a cause for feeling guilty. Buying yourself something nice, taking time out, eating something 'sinful' or even having a few hours extra sleep can all give rise to this emotion.

Guilt demands self-punishment and as such is resentment in disguise. It is resentment towards ourselves. Some writers even suggest that it is more than just being 'not of God'; it is even a form of an attack on God. Certainly it is a major block to both our personal and spiritual growth. The emergence of our deeper Self comes to a standstill as long as we are holding onto guilt. It may even be a form of manipulation; by punishing ourselves we are also indirectly hurting others whom we are depriving of our best Self.

The God of the New Testament is presented as a loving and merciful Father. The three well-known parables in Luke 15, telling of the Lost Sheep, the Lost Coin and the Lost Son all portray forgiveness as not just for the sinner, but we also see the Father's delight at receiving back what was always his in the first place. There is even the suggestion that he only forgives from the perspective of the sinner. From his own perspective he doesn't need to, since he never condemned in the first place.

The delicate interplay between guilt and resentment finds expression in the words from the Lord's Prayer, 'Forgive us our trespasses as we forgive those who trespass against us'. Again this is taken up in Matthew 18 where Peter begins with the question, 'If I am wronged, how often must I forgive?' Jesus goes on to tell a parable about a servant who is brought before his king for being unable to pay off a huge debt. In his mercy the king cancels the debt. Not long after, that same servant refuses to forgive someone who owed him a tiny sum. He even tries to do violence to him. Then the master apparently reverses his earlier decision and has the servant put in prison until he pays back everything that he owes. Prison here is very symbolic of the state of mind which resentment can create.

From this parable we can take for granted that there is a direct co-relation between our need to live in the awareness of Divine Mercy and of our own need to be merciful. When it comes to our need to forgive there are two extremes, we can forgive too quickly or we can hold onto the resentment for too long and not forgive at all.

To forgive too quickly has the inherent danger of not recognizing the extent of hurt and bypassing our feelings of anger. Many necessary stages of the human journey are bypassed when we rush into a forgiving mode. It can be a form of placing a spiritual bandage around a psychological problem, and there is a huge price to pay. The repressed feelings become part of our Shadow and until they are acknowledged this can result in a host of problems like depression, anxiety and irritability. Eventually these issues, if not expressed, may only find expression through our body tissues and result is various forms of psychosomatic diseases. Forgiveness finds its rightful place, never at the beginning, but at the end of a process. This process is one of self-discovery. The one hurt may have awakened earlier memories that also have to be dealt with. However, once the process is complete, forgiveness is an absolute requirement. This need not necessarily come because the other party deserves it, but it is granted because I deserve it. I do so in order to free myself. Forgiveness, when it does happen, is that special moment in time, when I release myself from the darkness of the past and give to myself the promise of a bright new future. This in turn may pave the way for reconciliation with the other party.

Grievances – The unhappy ever after saga!

Nursing grievances is a sure recipe for 'living unhappily ever after'. A grievance is when our ego hijacks our minds, takes us to hell, demands a ransom, and still leaves us there! No grievance, no matter how justified it appears, is worth holding onto; it costs too much and it is just not worth the baggage of pain, hate and fear that goes with it. To carry a grievance is to seek revenge and seeking revenge is like digging two holes; one for the person we are annoyed with and the other for ourselves. The bombs of anger, resentment and hate can only be carried within our own minds and there they must explode, hurting us first before they can hurt anyone else. A grievance also makes us see ourselves as victims and in that victim mode we leave ourselves vulnerable to attracting other people and circumstances into our lives that will inevitably victimize us and confirm how we are thinking about ourselves. The unforgiving mind uses anger for energy, fear to navigate and pain to judge everything by. A grievance is never a solution to a problem, but forgiveness is. Forgiveness alone can switch us from fear to love, pain to peace, past to present and despair to freedom.

How do I forgive?

When we say that we can't forgive, what we usually mean is that we won't forgive, or that we refuse to forgive. The primary requirement for forgiveness is an act of will. Where that willingness is missing we may have to first surrender our unwillingness to the Lord in order to receive it as a grace. Forgiveness is not a technique; it needs no expertise and surprisingly, no effort. Intention is what really matters, we only make way for forgiveness and then it takes on a life of its own and works for us. It is a form of wisdom in action and the more we practise it the more our spirit wings will grow stronger. The key point to remember is:

>'Whenever I forgive anyone it sets me free.'

Forgiven and Forgiving

When we are stricken and cannot bear our lives any longer,
Then a tree has something to say to us.
'Be still, be still.
Look at me, life is not easy, life is not difficult'
These are childish thoughts.
Let God speak within you, and your thoughts will grow silent.
You are anxious because your path leads away from mother and home.
But, every step and every day, leads you back again to the mother.
Home is neither here nor there.
Home is either within you,
or home is nowhere at all.
HERMAN HESSE

11

The Suffering Self

It's Yew – It's You!

Yew Vases

The above pieces originated in the Presidential garden at Áras An Uachtaráin in Dublin's Phoenix Park. Thankfully I didn't have to breach security to cut down one of the trees! Both vases are made from yew, which is one of the oldest trees in Europe. But, it is yew with a difference, and a difference that makes such pieces unique and highly sought after. On numerous occasions, I have been asked to sell these two vases and simply name the price. Each time I have managed to resist the temptation. With pale yellows and dark greens, brilliant reds and dark browns, these are pieces of exquisite beauty that offer an amazing variation both in colours and patterns.

My first encounter with this very different yew came about by accident. While cutting the log, from which the two pieces were made, I noticed sparks flying off the electric saw blade. I discovered that a piece of wire had been tied around the tree at a much younger age and rather than be limited in its growth, or choked by this offending article, the branch had managed to grow around it and incorporate it into its substance. The wonderful array of internal colours convinced me that any pieces made from the log were destined to be 'twins'. At the time this was a rather daunting task since I had only taken up woodturning a few months earlier

The Suffering Self

STRESSED YEW

The above are another few examples of this stressed or tortured yew, which I found among my woodpile. Again we have the beautiful grain configurations, but in these pieces the colour is much darker with small amounts of bright yellow. The centre-piece of the small mushroom inside the larger can symbolize the wounded or traumatized parts of the personality, or the vulnerable ones in society that require special care. Also, here it is possible to see the contrast between the ordinary wood and the yew that has been constricted but responded to the challenge in order to survive.

How these beautiful colours and intricate grain pattern had come about was a matter that intrigued me. I initially presumed that they had come as a consequence of rust from the wire being absorbed by the wood and discolouring it. A learned botanist has since informed me that this is only a small part of what happens. The bigger picture is that when subjected to the stress of a foreign body, over which it has no control, the wood itself undergoes a series of chemical reactions that transforms its cellular structure and allows it to incorporate this life-threatening object into itself. The process is somewhat similar to the response of the oyster when it is subjected to an offensive grain of sand. It cannot get rid of it, so it begins to secrete a substance around it, and this eventually forms a pearl.

It goes without saying that this 'stressed' yew which has undergone such a process, and triumphed over adversity, is much more interesting and valuable than wood which has never had to face such a challenge. Applying the same principle to life, those who have suffered, and have had to overcome severe handicaps and life threatening challenges, have an extra special quality, which gives them a unique depth of character, with a beauty that sets them in a class of their own.

So the message of this wonderful wood is:

'It's not just Yew; it's You!'

Special Olympics 2003

Olympic Torch

The previous chapter was first published as 'A Woodturner's Tribute' to all the athletes taking part in the Special Olympics of June 2003. The lamp is a version of the Olympic Torch that, in the words of Nelson Mandela who opened the games, represents, 'The triumph of the human spirit'. The World Summer Games were hosted by Ireland and involved eight thousand participants and thirty thousand volunteers. It was the first time that the games were ever held outside of the U.S.A.

12

Treasure from the Deep

Transforming the Unacceptable

Ornate Rose Bowl

This rose bowl is designed around the finial feature on the cover. Beech is used for the surrounds while purple heart makes up the main body. Both are seen in their natural colours, with the vivid red of the purple heart in striking contrast with the lighter coloured beech. The purple heart used here, and elsewhere in the collection, has an interesting history that has symbolic overtones. The wood is estimated to be at least six to seven hundred years old, which set in context means that it was already part of a mature tree when Columbus set sail for America in 1492. It originated in the Amazon Rain Forest. Since it is denser than water, and therefore impervious to it, it was once used extensively in shipbuilding, wharfs and as props for mine shafts.

Wood from the Sea

The piece shown is an end cut from the original timber shortly after it was recovered from the sea. For many years local fishermen in the area of Kilmore Quay had been dragging to the surface some very ugly and strange looking pieces of timber that had become fouled in their nets. Having no apparent value, and seeing no use for it, they treated it as an encumbrance, and quickly dispatched it back to the deep. Knowing my interest in woodturning, and curious to see if anything of beauty could be made from this very hard wood, one of them kept a few pieces on board his boat for me to collect. The striking colours found beneath the dark, barnacle-crusted exterior were quite wonderful and even though they tend to darken with time, they still retains a rich beauty.

Inlay Chalice & Paten

An unusual feature of the pieces being picked up was, that while some were obviously much older than others, and all bore the marks of sea worms, most of them were quite uniform in size and shape. This called for some research that led me to a man who, while growing up, had been friendly with an old sailor, long since dead. This sailor, he remembered, used to tell stories from his grandfather's time, of shiploads of such cargo being brought from Brazil to Wales, for use in the mining industry. According to his account, women and children loaded these logs that were in lengths suitable for use in the mineshafts. This was during the early days of the Industrial Revolution, which would be in the 1820s to 1840s. Many ships floundered along the South Coast of Ireland, particularly in the rough seas of the Tuskar Rock region. This meant that each piece recovered had been at the bottom of the sea for nearly two hundred years. What was even more remarkable after all the years was to find that the original sap was still evident in the wood.

NECKLACE BOWL

The story of the Purple Heart wood contains all the ingredients of a modern parable:

'A fisherman went out to fish. When he reached his favourite spot, he cast his net as he always did. Sometime later, as he hauled it on board, he felt a heaviness that made him quiver with the excitement of making a good catch. Much to his disappointment, all he took on board was a small quantity of fish and in their midst was a large piece of very black, slimy and ugly looking timber! On so many occasions before, he had been fooled in this way and each time feeling annoyed, he had quickly consigned the offending piece back to the deep. Still feeling cheated, he was about to do what he had done so often before when he stopped, looked at the piece of wood and began to wonder where it had come from; after all trees don't grow in the ocean! How long had it been submerged? Was it part of a shipwreck of a bygone era? Had lives been lost? What was its history? The questions detained him long enough for the piece to receive a stay of execution. On his home trip the piece was still in the bottom of the boat and beginning to dry out under the warm sun. To fill in the time he took from his pocket a penknife and began to cut beneath the surface. To his amazement the most vivid colours of red, purple and yellow began to appear. Coming ashore, he went with haste to a local craftsman who, on examining the wood, was able to answer many of his questions and inform him that the most valuable part of his catch for

the day was not his fish, but the piece of wood. Naturally he thought of so many other days when, out of ignorance and annoyance, he had brought home only fish.

Viewed symbolically, the sea, with all its mystery is a powerful symbol of the unconscious. The unconscious is the part of ourselves that continually surprises us with the particular people, circumstances and events it can bring to the surface in our lives. Often there is a recurring pattern to what it produces and, like the fisherman dumping his logs, the temptation is to dispose of whatever surfaces as quickly as possible. For example, if a particular kind of person again and again comes into my life with whom I always end up in conflict, he or she may be teaching me what I least want to hear, but most need to know about myself. It may take many years and a trail of broken relationships, before I resist using the scissors treatment once again on someone and stay with the relationship long enough to see what it has to teach me.

Losing a job, or seeing a business that I have given my heart and soul to for years go to the wall, is a matter of deep disappointment, but at a deeper level there may be a sense of relief, which is hard to understand. I may have been doing something purely for the sake of the money and now the redundancy carries the possibility of getting involved in something more fulfilling and creative. Similarly a business can literally take over my life and soul to the extent that it becomes synonymous with my identity. Christ once spoke of the danger of having gained the world but at the expense of one's soul (Luke 9:25). The loss and pain at one level, carries within it the possibility of a real gain that is ultimately far more important.

Sickness or disease, represent another unwelcome intrusion from the unconscious. The particular symptom may carry a profound message, but if there is a possibility of having it removed I will tend to take that avenue as quickly as possible. It could be the common cold, which may be a reminder that I am too busy, and need to take care of myself. Or, it may be something much more serious, like cancer which on the surface appears to be life threatening, but at a deeper level may be the greatest wake up call to become whole that I have ever received in my life.

Advice from an Angel

The Book of Tobit is one of the least known books of the Old Testament. It is an exquisite story containing some beautiful symbolism of how healing can be found in the most unexpected places. Tobit is a devout and God fearing Israelite living in exile in Nineveh around 721B.C. One day he is sleeping in his courtyard with his face uncovered, when sparrow droppings fall into his eyes causing him to lose his sight. His world falls apart and he feels that his life is coming to an end. He remembers that he has money deposited at Rages in Media that he would like his son Tobias to have. The story centers around the journey to Rages to recover this money. It is undertaken by Tobias and a travelling companion, who later reveals himself to be Raphael, the Angel of Healing.

The pair set off and after a day's travelling Tobias goes to wash his feet in the Tigris river, when a giant fish suddenly attacks him. Raphael orders him to seize the fish and remove its gall, heart and liver because they make 'useful medicines'. What they need of the flesh can then be eaten.

The action of seizing the fish is deeply symbolic in the broadest sense of the overall journey to healing and wholeness. The fish can be seen as something threatening, suddenly arising from the depths, and putting life at risk. The advice of the angel is to lay hold of the creature, rather than be devoured by it or run away in fear. Also they are to take nourishment from it. This is the first major step towards healing. Facing the truth that appears so unacceptable, and extracting what is good from something so terrifying, is an enormous challenge. Yet it contains hope and the potential for bringing good even out of evil.

Towards the end of the story, when Tobias arrives home, he smears the gall from the fish on Tobit's eyes and he is then able to peel away the cataracts and his father's vision is restored.

An interesting detail of the story is that Tobias has a dog that insists on following them on the journey. From a psychological perspective the 'dog' is an important figure and can represent the Shadow or dark, instinctual side of human nature. Many commentators would argue that the older Church with its pursuit of perfection, tried to lock up 'the dog' and failed to see him as having any place on the journey.

For example, the repression of the 'shadow', especially in the area of sexuality, has, to a large extent, contributed to its unwelcome expression in the form of abuse. In this respect sexual abuse, while a major problem that has to be dealt with in itself, can also be understood as a symptom. It draws attention to, and cries out for healing of a deeper malady, the disowned sexual shadow of God's people. The Shadow will always be a part of us; the 'dog' will always insist on following, whether he is made welcome or not!

13

Getting a Balance

Being and Doing

The Wheel of Life

The piece shown is a platter made from Monkey Puzzle. The branches of darker colours radiate outwards both at uniform height and angles from each other. A cross section of the tree can closely resemble a wheel with spokes and a rim. The inner core of the tree is usually either soft or hollow and the inserted piece completes the picture of a wheel with a hub.

Reflected in the piece is the ancient idea of the Wheel of Life. According to this concept the hub of the wheel is Spirit, which could also be termed 'Self'. The spokes represent the different aspects of life that must be kept in balance in order for the wheel to function. In the piece shown there are five spokes which at the outer level could be understood as areas like family, relationships, work, recreation and learning. At the inner level they can equally represent different personality types and the way they compliment each other

Spirit or Self as the hub of the wheel represents the importance of being in right relationship with oneself and with God. The faster the wheel spins the more essential it is that the hub be secure. If someone is off centre with themselves they cannot be on centre with anyone or anything else. The hub is also the part that requires lubrication. Where this is not given through reflection, meditation and prayer the result is friction and being in conflict with others. The wheel can only revolve around the hub of this important concept.

As the pace of life increases we tend to live our lives responding to the urgent demands of everyday living, often to the detriment of the issues that are important. It is common experience that urgent demands always present themselves as being very important, while the truly important ones never seem quite so urgent, and can so can easily get postponed. This may continue for a considerable time until eventually we find ourselves in the middle of a crisis, where the wheel no longer turns or stands in danger of collapse. A crisis in Chinese understanding is 'a dangerous opportunity' where we are faced with a choice, and we either make serious changes and get back on the road or suffer complete breakdown.

The wheel is self-contained which captures the idea that the energy we need for living is limited. To over invest in one area can only be done at the expense of another. Someone with a need to prove themselves may give an inordinate commitment to work and for a long time be blind to the reality that their circle of friends is getting smaller and, if in a relationship, that their partner is forced to live an almost single life. The crisis in such cases is often that the wife or partner gets involved with someone else and this becomes a 'wake up call' to examine what is really going on.

Tony grew up in a home where he was often told that he would never be good for anything. He married a lovely girl and for the first two years they were blissfully happy living in a mobile home. Building his own home became Tony's big chance to prove himself. He worked every available hour to the extent that it became an obsession. His wife often reminded him how driven he had become and how they now spent so little time together. What bit they did have was usually spent talking about the house. As she fell deeper into loneliness and depression, Tony continued to justify his actions by saying that everything he was doing was for her and their future family. Two years later the dream house was complete. Sadly they moved in as strangers and tragically it never became a home. Just six months later she became involved with someone else and shortly afterwards they went their separate ways.

For the person who is losing their partner to someone else there is inevitably a strong sense of anger and injustice. They will conveniently adopt the common understanding of adultery that usually centers only on sexual infidelity. It's true meaning reaches much deeper and sees adultery as anything that acts as a wedge in the primary relationship between partners which forces them apart. The concept of sexual infidelity is included in this understanding but it is seen more as the end result of a separation process. Viewed in this light, so many areas such as work, hobbies, sport or even children, could, with over investment, act as an adulterous wedge. It takes great courage and honesty for the aggrieved party to admit that by their neglect of the important spoke of their relationship, they were driving the wedge and setting the scene for their partner's infidelity.

Reg was an elderly man who reacted very angrily when I referred in a talk to adultery as a 'wedge'. I took his verbal abuse on the chin sensing that the message had struck a sensitive chord. Thirty minutes later, and with tears in his eyes, he admitted that his wife had lived and died a lonely woman because of his obsession with a hobby that he had allowed to take precedence over everything else in his life. His sense of pride that he had never in his life been unfaithful to her had been shattered and shooting the messenger rather than facing the truth was far easier.

Personality Types

Much of Carl Jung's life was devoted to describing the whole or total human being. Part of his unique contribution was to ascribe different categories to the range of personality types. The most basic category is that of *'extrovert'* and *'introvert'*. These are terms which have now become part of everyday language. The extroverts gravitate towards the outer world and are energized by their dealings with it. The introverts are more at home with the inner world and find their energy from within. Most people are well developed in one area of life at the expense of the other. Yet without inner development, the life of the extrovert may be shallow, and without being able to function in the outer world, the introvert becomes isolated and his wisdom never comes to fruition. An essential part of the journey of life is to develop both inwardly and outwardly. Both spokes of the wheel need to be looked after in order to foster wholeness.

Another two categories are *thinking* and *feeling*. The first arrives at conclusions by means of abstract thought, while the other, by recourse to feeling, will make their judgment. Where a situation calls for a feeling response, the feeling type person is at their best but where a thinking process is called for, such a person is dealing with their inferior side. Again, without an attempt being made to integrate both spokes, wholeness is not possible.

The final two categories are *sensation* and *intuition*. Sensation here is understood as what brings us facts and information and what puts us in touch with the so called 'real' world. These are the people who are eminently practical, who tend to be good at business and are experts in the art of everyday living. The world of the intuitive is also very real but has a different quality. Both are good at perceiving reality, but in different ways. Intuition is about 'seeing around corners' and as such is much more intangible and elusive. It is the sensing of realities not visible to the senses. Jung describes it as 'unconscious perception'. As with the other categories, an over identification with one, to the detriment of the other, is not the path to becoming a complete human being.

Mid-Life Balance

It is well worth remembering that the first half of life is spent developing extroversion *or* introversion, thinking *or* feeling, sensation *or* intuition. Consequently, over identification is inevitable. An essential part of Jung's thought was that as we enter into the second half of life we find energy and enthusiasm, not from what we were good at before, but from developing those aspects of ourselves which were earlier ignored. For the ancient wheelwrights, balancing the wheel was an essential part of their craft, and it is equally true in the psychological sphere.

Maintaining a proper balance between all the different spokes of life and between responding to the urgent, yet not neglecting the important, is an ongoing struggle that needs constant monitoring and readjustment. It requires among other things, an ability to be ones own person, to say, 'No' occasionally, to maintain proper boundaries and have a facility to listen to significant others when they try to tell us that a better balance is needed. When we don't listen, and choose denial instead of reality, then sooner or later fate comes knocking at our door and we have no option but to open it. It may well be that in our darkest, lowest moments we will come to appreciate the words of St. John of the Cross when he said, 'In the darkness we may see things more clearly than we do in the light'!

14

Embracing Assertiveness

A Matter of Respect

Passivity – Lack of respect for myself

Passivity

The piece resembles a gentle Medieval mace-head where the points don't really want to cause any damage. Any contact causes them to drop back into their holes. When the ball is moved, the points on the underside fall forwards and point out, reflecting the inner aggression that will inevitably find expression, while those on the upper surface retreat into their holes and are almost hidden. This provides an excellent symbol of the passive individual who is ultra sensitive and never wants to cause offence or harm but internalizes everything at the expense of their own respect and selfhood.

The person who adopts a passive way of behaving can be identified by many of the following characteristics:

A *'doormat syndrome'*, where they continually let themselves be walked on and have other people leave their 'dirt' behind. The question that has to be asked here is, if someone sees themselves as a doormat do they really have the right to complain?

Being *'non confrontational'*. Not standing up for their rights and allowing others to get away with unacceptable behaviour. The problem with this approach is that whenever we avoid an issue which needs to be addressed, we lose our self-esteem.

'Avoidance of responsibility' for making choices. Leaving decision making to others.

'Making excuses' for others behaviour. This prevents the people from coming to maturity and taking responsibility for their lives. Something may be understandable but it doesn't make it excusable. Childish behaviour, which is always excused, is never likely to change.

'Peace at all costs' is not a genuine peace and is purchased at the high cost of a lot of inner turmoil. Similarly the approach of 'anything for a quiet life' is to internalize the outer aggression, and leave oneself prone to suffering depression.

Being *'non-defensive'* and taking everything that is thrown at you. This suggests that the person is lacking in self-forgiveness and accepts everything as a form of punishment.

Playing the *'helpless victim'* where outside forces always dictate my life. Here others always hold power without any realization on my part that they only have as much power as I have given them.

'Acting the Martyr' where I just 'grin and bear it'. Suffering is carried in silence with a vague hope that one day all I have done will be recognized, perhaps not in this life, but hopefully in the life to come.

Passive people can also be *'quite manipulative'*. Lacking the courage to ask directly for what they want, they try to get it indirectly. This they do by playing games or making people feel guilty.

The consequences for the personality of being too passive are serious in the extreme. Self-worth is continually being eroded; anger is being internalized, with ensuing inner conflict. There is a build-up of tension resulting in mood swings. What is not being said, but needs to be said, creates a barrier of communication and this results in feelings of isolation. Eventually the body is likely to express in terms of sickness what the passive individual has never had the courage to say, with the physical disease reflecting the internal dis-ease or lack of ease with what has been going on for so many years.

Aggression – Lack of respect for the other

Aggression

This time the piece shown is a Medieval mace with the obvious symbolism of being threatening, defensive and destructive. The colours used are those we associate with anger, red and black. Also the base has the profile of two faces in a head to head confrontation. As such it provides a very powerful symbol of the aggressive person who commands attention but is lacking in both being able to give and receive love.

Many of the following characteristics identify the aggressive personality:

'Shoot first and ask questions afterwards'. Hasty conclusions are reached on the basis of feelings alone, without seeking out the truth. They tend to act both compulsively and destructively without taking the consequences into consideration. The result is that the other person often finds himself or herself wounded for an offence they were totally unaware of and certainly hadn't intended.

'A desire to seek revenge'. This is a 'get even' mentality where evil is repaid with evil, much like the Old Testament philosophy of, 'An eye for an eye and a tooth for a tooth'. As Mark Twain once pointed out, this can only result in everyone becoming blind and toothless! A further consequence of repaying evil with evil is that if the reaction is as bad as the original action, then the victim is revealing himself to be every bit as malicious as the person he holds responsible for the offence.

'Seeing only one side of the story'. This is invariably one's own side, where there is a reluctance to face the multi-faceted dimension of truth. With the aggressive personality there may be a willingness to hear, but not always an openness to listen, to the other person's point of view. The age-old wisdom that every story has three sides; yours, mine and the truth, is largely ignored.

'Explosive outbursts'. Here insult is added to injury with offensive and abusive language being used. Words are spoken which cannot be unsaid. Voices are raised, fingers are pointed in accusation, fists are clenched with rage and eyes glare in anger. The scene is all too familiar. The instinctive response when treated in such a manner is to defend oneself and to retaliate with the possibility of resolution becoming less and less likely.

'Always needing to be right and to come out on top'. They must get their own way no matter what. Having the last word in every argument is important for the aggressive individual. Usually they are more interested in being right than being in relationship.

'Abusive, intolerant, blaming and judgmental' are words, which often characterize the person in the aggressive mode. They tend to be continuously embroiled in outer conflict, which mirrors their own inner turmoil. Enemies are easily made and they tend to bring out the worst in others. When called upon to deal with difficult situations their approach makes them more part of the problem than the solution, and so they leave behind a trail of unresolved issues and unfinished business. Having antagonized others by getting their way aggressively, they usually find themselves isolated and suffering the loneliness which comes from being constantly at war with oneself.

Assertiveness – Respect for Self and Others

Assertiveness

This piece stands taller than the other two since it occupies the midpoint of the scale and represents the goal we are aiming for. It is a plug-cut sphere. The boundary wall is firm, while the inner core is flexible. The cut-through holes intersect, representing the capacity to take in and give out. The finial on top represent the capacity to be single minded about the commitment to be true to oneself, and to the fulfillment of one's own destiny.

While assertive people give respect both to themselves and to others, they also command respect and receive it in large quantities. This enables then to continuously grow in self-esteem and confidence. While they expect the best from others, they usually receive it, since they also have the capacity to draw it forth.

In situations of conflict the assertive individual is not so concerned about who is right or wrong, but rather who is hurting. They have a great capacity for justice and are able not just to hear, but also to listen to all sides of a story and reach decisions based on reasoned judgment. Recognizing that they never know the full truth, they tend to judge actions rather than people, and so others find them open, flexible, accommodating and understanding.

Recognizing their own needs, and asking openly and directly for what they want, is an important aspect of assertiveness, as is recognizing and respecting the rights and needs of others.

Assertive people usually have healthy and creative ways of expressing their anger. They tend to wait until they can speak their truth in love rather than simply love to speak the truth out of anger. When genuinely hurt, they tend to take personal responsibility for their feelings and use 'I' statements rather than the 'you' of accusation. The result is that they tend to have few, if any, enemies but lots of admirers. Their manner of dealing with conflict tends to deepen their personal relationships and often wins them life-long friends.

Their assertive approach to life makes them powerful agents for growth and change. Because their truth on various issues is spoken without malice or anger it has the effect of being heard. When they have to confront those who are guilty of unacceptable behaviour, those spoken to usually feel respected as persons, and often experience a change of heart, which gives them a new direction in life. Having been respected themselves they have also had the opportunity to learn respect for others

The Passive Aggressive

PASSIVE~~~~~~~~~~~~~~~~~ASSERTIVE~~~~~~~~~~~~~~~~~AGGRESSIVE

While passivity and aggressiveness stand at different poles, we may find ourselves at both extremes, being passive-aggressive. Having absorbed too much negative energy and suffered abuse for too long, the tide begins to turn, and we frighten ourselves when we eventually let loose and express what we had held inside for so many years. Living with someone who is passive-aggressive is like walking through a minefield. Even though the path seems perfectly clear, there are certain spots that if stepped on will set off an explosion.

In our need to develop an assertive approach, after discovering that we have been too passive, we invariably come across as aggressive. The pendulum having been released from one extreme, will naturally swing to the other, before slowly coming to rest midway in the space we call assertiveness. Another common case scenario is for someone to be both passive and aggressive in different situations. The 'street angel and house devil' is a typical example of this. At work a man may be as meek as a lamb, and when he goes home acts like a tyrant.

For the unfolding of the true Self towards the fullness of personhood, the quality of assertiveness is both a necessary goal and a vital component.

16

Birth Scripts – Life Scripts.

What Was or What Is?

Birthing

Birth Legacies

The enfolding shape of this vase, made from yew, suggests femininity, the womb and giving birth. As we grow in self-understanding we sometimes find that certain personality characteristics, difficulties we have in relationships, or problems with our emotional life can seem to have such a direct co-relation with the manner of our birth, that to a large extent our birth script has become our life script. In recent years, techniques based on breathing and relaxation have been developed which can unlock those memories buried deep in the unconscious and put us in touch again with what happened on that momentous day we were born. The theory behind such techniques is that memory doesn't just belong to the domain of the brain, but is distributed throughout our bodies in the minerals within our cells.

Rebirth

At a certain stage during my own training as a psychotherapist, exposure to this technique helped dispel one of my deepest fears and throw light on a question that I had often wondered about. For many years I had suffered a fear of abandonment, that if ever a real crisis came into my life I would be left utterly alone. Also, a sense I had carried with me for so long was that I had been born without feeling. While attending a workshop I was able to regress to the experience of my birth, and find that after three days of labour my mother just gave up from exhaustion. This I experienced as abandonment. Then a doctor was called who administered an anesthetic, which passed from my mother into me. The birth process was then completed, but I was born without feeling. Luckily my mother was still alive at the time, and able to confirm every detail of what had transpired

Many aspects of our lives may have been affected by the manner of our birth? Some of our problems could have either stemmed from our birth, or been exacerbated by it. Our birth script may leave us with a predisposition to respond to life in a particular manner. Whether we go down that particular path will depend on a myriad of other factors. Set out below is a list of many different kinds of birth, with their possible repercussions. Reflecting on the birth scenario, most of the conclusions reached by research could also be arrived at by applying common sense and logic. An example of this is one who has had a Caesarean birth. After being disturbed in the womb, such a person is likely in later life to have a dislike of being disturbed.

Rapid Birth resulting in shock and trauma.
Feeling of having missed out on something.
Unfulfilled. Always chasing after something else and something better.
Being success and achievement driven. Always striving for more.
Emptiness deep inside, and not knowing what one is looking for.
Rushing headlong into things.

Induced Birth. Artificially started and controlled.
Not able to trust people.
Not able to get started.
Always feeling controlled.
Never feeling ready. 'Don't push me!'
Easily bullied and abused.
Reluctance to speak up for myself.
Suffering from the 'door mat syndrome'.
Feeling downtrodden.
Suffering from fears and holding onto tension.

Gender Disappointment. Parents wanting a child of the opposite sex.
All future relationships feel wrong because of the first disappointment.
Falls in and out of love easily and enjoys the chase. Flirtatious.
Problems with commitment.

Fears around having children.
Feeling inadequate as a man or woman.
Identity problems.
Envy. Comparing myself with others.
Being a tomboy or effeminate.

Caesarean Birth.
Disliking touch, not able to be tactile.
Feeling misunderstood and angry with life.
Not liking to be disturbed.
Tendency to procrastinate.
Not able to follow through on projects.
Expecting things to be done for you.
Not putting effort into things.
Always falling on your feet.

Forceps Birth or Vacuum Extraction.
Feeling powerless throughout life.
Lack of motivation.
Difficulty with making decisions.
Problems with headaches.
Anger, helplessness and constant worry.
Stress related illnesses.
'Why can't I do anything on my own?'

Breech Birth – Struggle.
Feeling a victim.
Finding it hard to do things the right way round.
Backing out when under pressure.
Stress and stress-related health problems.
Always feeling that life is a struggle.

Born with cord around neck.
Dislike of anything around neck, e.g. Scarves or Ties.
Fear of suffocation.
Tightness around the neck.

Premature Birth.
Always looking ahead. Living in the future
Tendency to pass oneself by.
Being early for appointments.
Not staying with emotions.

Drugged Birth.
Never feeling fully alive without stimulation.
Always in a fog.
Yawning a lot.
Fading in and out. Not able to stay fully alert.
Often equate support with suffocation.
Sometimes finding it hard to focus.
Feeling out of touch and disconnected in relationships.
Out of touch with feelings. 'Emotionally cold'.
Sense of being 'spaced out'
Suppressing of emotions.
Tendency to equate separation with loss.
Addictive tendencies.
Abandonment anxiety.

False Labour.
Tendency in life to make false starts.

16

Transformation of the Self

'Do not conform, but be transformed'
Romans 12:2

Dinosaur in Bog Oak

The above piece, made from bog oak, has been preserved in an Irish bog for at least five thousand years. As such, it is a carrier of enormous history. It is a piece for which I have a special affinity, being my first excursion into the field of carving and working with bog oak. Looking at this piece people see different things; perhaps a pheasant, or a bird of paradise. The original piece, although rough, crumbly, crusty, even ugly, was still a most interesting specimen of wood. My original reaction was to ask myself what was I going to make of it? For some reason, I started to reflect on the question and sensed that this approach was in some way offensive to the wood. I then changed the question to, what does this piece want to become? It was a question which reminded me of Michelangelo looking at a block of marble and saying, 'There is a lion in there trying to come out'. Thousands of years ago, this piece had been a thing of beauty, and once again there was a possibility that a new beauty could be born. The wood was inviting me, not to try and conform it into my image, but to facilitate the emergence of its own uniqueness. I began work with the sense that I was obliged to this wood; it was not obliged to me. Although slightly abstract in form, the piece trying to emerge seemed to be a cross between a dinosaur and a bird. Viewed from the front it had the appearance of an ancient reptile, and from the back it had a distinct birdlike appearance. One species having evolved from the other in the distant past, and now being brought together in this piece of ancient wood, seemed to be the perfect expression of its utter uniqueness.

The unlived life of parents has the greatest influence on their children

When we are not allowed to be who we really are we start becoming someone else. The journey towards wholeness, or becoming my own unique Self, is one that is often at variance with the collective norms of society. There may be parental pressure to shape children into preconceived moulds. This may range from parents wanting a child of the other sex, to expecting the child to be like another sibling, or to influence the child to embrace a path in life that is not unique for them. What they are seeking is rather the fulfillment of their own unrealized ambitions. Many a child has to wear an overcoat just because the mother is cold! Parents, who are lacking in awareness, will unconsciously project their own fears, hurts and insecurities onto their children. Wherever there is unlived life in a parent, it can express itself in needing the child to conform. This limits the child's freedom to be truly who he or she really is. Much rebellion in children and adolescents may have its roots in the need to break free of the burden of conformity imposed by parents.

To educate is to draw forth

The ancient philosopher Socrates said that the function of education was to act as a midwife, drawing forth something that was already there. The word 'educate' comes from the Latin 'educare' which means 'to draw forth'. Most current educational systems emphasize just one form of intelligence, to the detriment of all others. Children with high mental ability are rewarded with points and degrees, while others, who may be quite brilliant in other fields, are left feeling second-class. The expectation is to conform and then to be rewarded. Not to conform, is to invite rejection.

Collective Expectations

Society in general is continually asking us to sacrifice our individuality on the altar of collectivity. The world of advertising survives on this principle. There is a continual onslaught of messages that suggest that happiness, fulfillment, and acceptance can only be found by using certain products or services. The range of implications of what it takes to be a fully alive human being is enormous. Our bodies have to be a particular shape, the house we live in has to be of a certain standard, we must be well qualified, perform meaningful work, socialize in certain circles and, most importantly, have lots of money. This list is endless and forms the basis of how society operates. Yet all the above are extraneous to our core identity. None of these things provide an answer to who we really are. An integral part of our inner journey may be to start questioning and challenging many of our deeply rooted and ingrained beliefs. To discover our own inner well, it may be necessary to admit that many other wells have failed to satisfy our thirst. At times like this, dreams often speak very powerfully of our need to be ourselves and break free of societal expectations, no matter what the cost. Collective dreams are those where I'm part of a large group, and often someone else is in charge. The implication is that I need to take charge and decide on my own path. Travelling on a train means to be running along rigid lines to a predetermined destination. Similarly being on a bus, a tram or being pushed along by the force of a crowd, all may indicate a need to stop conforming and make some radical, and even perhaps unpopular decisions, in order to reclaim my own identity.

Off-Centre Candlesticks

A pair of swans, gliding gracefully along a river, provided the inspiration for the above pieces. They are examples of 'off-centre' turning, and while both are very similar they are yet quite different. In a simple way they express the truth that unity is found in diversity, and true diversity is only possible where there is genuine uniqueness.

The Primary Vocation – Called to be Myself

'If a man does not keep step with his companions, perhaps it is because he hears a different drummer. Let him step to the music which he hears, however measured and far away.'

Thoreau

Each of us has an inner voice that encourages us to pursue our dreams, no matter what the cost; to take risks, and live life to the fullest. In contrast to the inner voice that whispers, there are other voices, outside us as well as within, and they shout different messages. They tell us to play it safe and be like everyone else. What if we fail, they ask; and if you are really going to be true to yourself, others may not like it, and you could end up being rejected. The inner voice belongs to our soul, as it encourages us to pursue our destiny. Each time we play the game of conformity, that voice will continue to plague us. The other voices are usually well intentioned, and often come from a position of love and genuine concern. They may even be the voice of experience. Yet while they represent the good in our lives they fall far short of the best. The conflict of our soul is rarely between good and evil, but more often between good and best. The cost of ignoring our soul's voice, and to honour our own drumbeat, is to condemn ourselves to frustration and mediocrity, where in the words of T.S. Eliott we must 'put on a face to meet the faces that we meet', as we live out lives of 'quiet desperation'.

'As he was walking along by the Sea of Galilee, Jesus watched two brothers Simon and Andrew casting a net into the sea. They were fisherman. He said to them, "Come follow me, and I will make you fishers of men.' (Matthew 4: 18-19)

In his work *The Development of Personality*, Carl Jung wrote:

> *'What is it in the end that induces a man to go his own way*
> *and to rise out of unconscious identity with the mass?*
> *It is what is commonly called vocation..........*
> *It acts like a law of God from which there is no escape.*
> *Anyone with a vocation hears the voice of the inner man:*
> *He is called'.*

Against the backdrop of the Second World War, Jung later wrote this extraordinary piece concerning the primacy and importance of individual transformation:

'The great events of world history are, at bottom, profoundly unimportant. In the last analysis, the essential thing is the life of the individual. This alone makes history; here alone do the great transformations take place, and the future, the whole history of the world, ultimately spring as a gigantic summation from these hidden sources in individuals. In our most private and most subjective lives we are not only the passive witnesses of our age, and its sufferers, but also its makers. We make our own epoch.'

17

True Self or False Self.

Thermometer or Thermostat?

Galileo Thermometer

The thermometer is based on the principle of Galileo Galilei who discovered that the density of a liquid is changed by varying temperatures. The temperature can be read from the disks hanging from the coloured spheres. These descend slowly when the temperature increases, and rise when the temperature falls. The lowest disk of the floating spheres indicates the current temperature. A thermometer reacts to the outside temperature, and rises or falls accordingly. A thermostat on the other hand works on a principle which is the very opposite. Instead of reacting to the outside environment, it effects the change, and determines the temperature.

Both of these instruments reflect two very different life principles or ways of being. One is to live a life of unawareness in a reactive mode. This is where one's inner life, happiness and sense of well-being is determined by outside forces. It is the place where we like to fool ourselves that the world 'out there' is the source of all our problems and only when that world is OK, can I begin to feel OK. The other is to be so in touch with the creative Self as to be able to change the outside environment. This is the place of recognizing that happiness is my responsibility alone, and that ultimately it is my inner reality, which is creating my outer reality. If I am continually attracting negative people and events into my life, which are causing me suffering, then it is something in me that is causing this to happen, and I can begin to do something about it.

REACTIVE
CREATIVE

These two contrasting principles can also be expressed in the two words 'reactive' and 'creative'. The number of letters in each word is exactly the same, as are the letters themselves. The main difference is in the placing of the 'c'. Ultimately it is how I 'see' that determines my response in any situation. One of the infallible signs of psychological maturity is where a person begins to take responsibility for their reactions, and recognize that they belong to them alone and are not infallible indicators of the truth. The danger is always to think that my reaction is the only appropriate way to behave in response to a particular situation, and be blind to the fact that someone else may respond in an entirely different manner.

Paying close attention to one's reactions in an ongoing manner is an exercise that pays rich dividends. It is our spontaneous and unrehearsed reactions that have the capacity to shed light into the dark realms of our unconscious and provide us with vital information which we may need in order to become whole. Whenever we find ourselves going 'over the top' on a particular issue, there is the tendency to excuse oneself as 'having a bad day' or dismiss it by saying, 'It wasn't really me'. This is to lose out on a vital gem of truth, and fail to make a connection with the part of me that it really is.

One day, Sandra's twenty-year-old son informed her that he was going to America for six months' work experience. She immediately broke down in tears and begged him not to leave her. Up to this he had left home on numerous occasions, while attending college, and a few times had travelled abroad. On none of these occasions did the mother indicate any reluctance about letting her son go. This time the 'dramatics' took everyone by surprise, none more so than Sandra herself. Talking through her reaction with a close friend, she suddenly remembered that at the age of three her father had died and instead of being told he had gone to Heaven, she was told that he had gone to America. Her reaction was revealing a deep childhood wound that was now crying out for attention.

When the thermometer principle is the prevailing one in our lives it is a strong indicator that we are living a surface existence, and out of touch with our true Self. This is when the ego or the false self is in charge and there will be numerous tell tale indicators:

- Needing approval and admiration from others.
- Constantly comparing myself with others.
- Not taking risks out of fear of failure, humiliation or rejection.
- Feeling anxious and fearful.
- Needing more and more outer stimulation.
- Disliking silence and avoiding my own company.
- Taking things personally.
- Taking myself too seriously and lacking a sense of humour.
- Blaming, criticizing and judging others.
- Being intolerant about others shortcomings.
- Not having a sense of Providence.
- Thinking that success and achievement are all important.
- Feeling hurried and driven.
- Needing always to be right.
- Resisting change.
- Being a perfectionist, where we take pains and give them to others!
- Needing to control and manipulate.
- Living with a tyranny of 'musts', 'shoulds' and 'oughts'.
- A desperate search for love and security.
- Needing to find the perfect person who will make me happy.
- Being competitive rather than being co-operative.
- Living in the past. Unable to be in the present moment.
- Over concern with outward appearance and worldly success.
- Addictive behaviour, needing 'a fix' for one's inner emptiness.
- Seeing happiness always in the future in terms of 'when' something happens.

Apart from the above, two of the strongest indicators that we are out of touch with our true selves is when we find ourselves playing the victim or the martyr. The difference is that while victims tend to live in the past, always blaming something or other, martyrs live in the future, when all their efforts will be recognized, and their heroics eventually rewarded.

There is no denying that 'victimhood' has its origins in specific incidents of victimization in the past and these unresolved issues make the person like a magnet for disaster where similar problems repeat themselves over and over again.

Victimhood tends to be characterized by 'if onlys'. If only my parents had been different; if only I had married someone else; if only I had chosen a different career. Whenever we find ourselves blaming circumstances, ancestry, partner, society, the government or God, for whatever is happening in our lives, then we are in victim mode and ultimately disempowering ourselves.

Martyrs believe that it is by suffering that they will get their reward. They put up with feeling the weight of the world, which they believe is being continually placed on their shoulders. Nobody shows them consideration or appreciation, yet they are always there for everyone else to dump their problems and demands on. Very rarely are they seen to complain, but they do have an amazing capacity to send other people on guilt trips. The anger of the martyr is silent, but it also seeks revenge. Making others feel guilty is their form of punishment.

While the thermometer is a useful symbol for the false or egocentric self, the thermostat is an equally good symbol of the true Self. The characteristics of this are very different to what is ego-generated and reflect a much deeper reality. They can include:

- *Wonder, awe and delight at the joy of being alive.*
- *A sense of humour where I carry myself lightly.*
- *Gratitude and joy.*
- *Not being burdened by fear and worry.*
- *Feeling complete in myself, yet in close communion with others.*
- *Being creative and having energy and enthusiasm.*
- *Taking responsibility for my life.*
- *Living in the present and having hope for the future.*
- *Feeling 100 per cent alive and alert.*
- *Having a sense of purpose and destiny.*
- *Being loving and forgiving towards others and myself.*
- *Living a balanced lifestyle.*
- *Being able to express feelings and opinions openly and honestly.*
- *Having a sense of Providence at work in my life.*
- *Having a sense of my own power.*
- *Knowing that I can make a difference.*
- *Seeing myself as forever growing and changing.*
- *Having respect for all things.*
- *Seeing the larger picture.*
- *Inner peace and harmony in relationships.*
- *Being content with the process rather than the goal.*

Grace – Effortless Power

From the world of golf comes a useful analogy for understanding the distinction between life lived at the level of Ego or False Self and living from the Higher Self. The harder and more effort a player puts into hitting a ball, the less likelihood it has of travelling any distance. With less effort and more rhythm, the ball performs at its best. Hence the saying, the secret of golf is, 'effortless power as opposed to powerless effort'. The Christian doctrine of Grace can also be viewed in the light of this principle. Grace can be understood as the availability of a higher power to live my life. An essential prerequisite and aspect of living the life of grace is surrender to the Divine. In psychological terms this can represent the Ego relinquishing control to the Self and entering into a new relationship with it. Perhaps one of the most dangerous travesties of the Christian religion is to reduce its message to the level of egocentric will-power where personal effort determines everything.

18

The Kingdom Within

The Hidden Treasure of the Self

Victorian Sovereign Holder

The piece shown is a Victorian Sovereign Box. On the surface it appears solid and impossible to open. Yet the mystery is that there is something rattling about inside. So how did it get in there in the first place? The question is answered in the second picture. This shows that by pressing one of the concentric circles a secret compartment is revealed which contains the coins.

A mysterious reality, central to the teaching of Jesus, was the Kingdom of Heaven. The importance of this is apparent from even glancing through the Gospels. Almost all his teachings are related to this concept. One could even say that he was obsessed with it. The phrase 'Kingdom of Heaven', is found in Matthew thirty-eight times, Mark thirteen and twenty eight times in Luke. Even in the Gospel of St. John, while it occurs only once, his constant use of the term 'eternal life ' has an equivalent meaning.

Twelve of St. Matthew's parables begin with the expression ' the Kingdom of Heaven is like…' One of them continues '…a treasure hidden in a field which someone has found; he hides it again, and goes off happy, sells everything he owns and buys the field'.
(Mt. 13:44)

Another says that 'the Kingdom is like a merchant looking for fine pearls: when he finds one of great value he goes and sells everything he owns and buys it'. (Mt. 3:45)

In the first case, something is discovered, apparently by accident, while a person is going about his everyday work. The second refers to someone who is actively involved in a search. In both cases a treasure is found which is of such immense value that it is worth giving up everything else in order to have it. This implies, that within each of us there is an inner reality like a great treasure hidden in the field of our soul, waiting to be discovered. Once it is uncovered, all other goals and ambitions are happily given up so that this treasure can become the central reality in one's life.

Individuation – Becoming Who I Really Am

Anyone familiar with the workings of the unconscious will recognize that there is a process at work within the individual, which is constantly promoting growth and seeking to bring about wholeness and fulfillment. Carl Jung coined a phrase for this mysterious force and called it, 'Individuation'. While it is always there, its success is by no means guaranteed since it is entirely dependent on co-operation from the Ego. Ultimately it is 'I' who decide the parameters of this process.

The two essential aspects of Individuation are growth and completion. These find expression in many Kingdom parables. In the one of the mustard seed, the seed grows to become a tree (Matthew 13:31). In another, the yeast which a woman mixes in the dough, causes the bread to rise to completion (Matthew 13:33). Both of these affirm the Kingdom as a reality in a person's life in the here and now. It is an agent for growth and brings about the unfolding, completion, and fulfillment of the personality. In other words it is not just a spiritual reality, but also a psychological one, in so far as the individual can experience it in the development of his or her personality.

The implications of this are profound:

- At the inner level the Kingdom is equivalent to the true Self. 'The Kingdom of Heaven is within you'. (Luke 17: 21)

- The challenge and the rewards of coming into a right relationship with the Self and of living out that relationship are expressed in Mark 6:33, 'Seek first the Kingdom and everything will be given you besides.' Divine Providence is a manifestation of inner harmony with the true Self.

- The coming of the Kingdom in each person's life is the unfolding of the Self. To truly pray, 'Thy Kingdom come', is to embrace the individuation process.

- While not taking from the transcendent nature of the Divinity, the search for the true Self is the same as the search for God, as the search for God is also a search for the Self. In the words of St. Clement of Alexandria, from the early Christian Church, 'He who knows himself knows God.'

- The authentic human journey towards wholeness *is* the authentic spiritual journey to God. Wholeness and holiness amount to the same thing. The only distinction between having a truly human life and having a spiritual life is purely academic.

- Any form of avoidance of our humanity is tantamount to Original Sin. 'We want to be like gods'. (Genesis 3:5). All authentic spirituality is grounded in the human reality. Pseudo spirituality and fundamentalism have a strong spiritual focus but are lacking in human awareness.

- The ultimate tragedy would be to gain the world i.e. fulfill one's egocentric goals, but suffer the loss of Self (Luke 9:25).

- Divinity in its humblest form is human, as in God becoming man, while the ultimate essence and dignity of being human, is to be divine, and have an eternal destiny.

Selected Bibliography for Volume One and Two

Collected Works	C. G. Jung	Pantheon Books '63

Adventures in Woodturning	David Springett	GMC Publications '94
Woodturning Wizardry	David Springett	GMC Publications '99
Woodturning Trickery	David Springett	GMC Publications '01
Masterful Woodturning	S. Gary Roberts	Sterling Publishing '00

Most Biblical quotations are taken from, *The Jerusalem Bible*, Doubleday and Co. '66

Urgings of the Heart	Wilkie Au & Noreen Cannon	Paulist Press '95
Living Magically	Gill Edwards	Piatkus '02
The Kingdom Within	John A. Sanford	Harper Collins '87
The Invisible Partners	John A. Sanford	Harper Collins '85
Mystical Christianity	John A. Sanford	Crossroad '94
Manifest Your Destiny	Wayne W. Dyer	Thorsons '98
Healing the Child Within	Charles L. Whitfield	Health Com. Inc. '87
Love is a Choice	Hemfelt, Minirith & Meir	Nelson '89
Co-Dependence	Ann Wilson Schaef	Harper Collins '86
Laughter the best Medicine	Robert Holden	Thorsons '93
Selected Poems	T.S. Eliott	Faber and Faber '54
Memories, Dreams and Reflections	C. G. Jung	Pantheon Books '63
Set Me Free	Henry Rohr	Spectrum '73
Healing the Family Tree	Kenneth Mc All	Sheldon '85
Your Inner Child Of the Past	W. Hugh Missildine	Simon & Schuster '90
The Psychology of Romantic Love	Robert A. Johnson	Penguin Arkana '83
Soul Psychology	Joshua David Stone	Light Technology '94
Anam Chara	John O'Donohue	Bantam Press '97
The Healing Power of Illness	Thorwald Dethlefsen	Element '91
Self Healing	Louis Proto	Piatkus '98
Our Inner Conflicts	Karen Horney	Norton '66
The Psychology of C. G. Jung	Jolande Jacobi	Yale '73
God and Patrick Kavanagh	Tom Stack	Columba '96
The Search for the Real Self	James Masterson	Free Press '90
The Undiscovered Self	C. G. Jung	R.K.P. '75
Man and Woman He Made Them	Jean Vanier	D. L. T. '86
The Bible and the Psyche	Edward F. Edinger	Inner City Books '85
The Christian Archetype	Edward F. Edinger	Inner City Books '87
The Symbolic Quest	E. Whitmont	Princeton '82
Individuation and Narcissism	Mario Jacobi	Routledge '84
Productive and Unproductive Depression	Emmy Gut	Routledge '92
Liberating the Heart	Lawrence W. Jaffe	Inner City '90
The Golden Key to Happiness	Masami Saionji	Element Books
Shift Happens	Robert Holden	Hodder and Stoughton '00
Signposts	Denise Linn	Rider Books '96
Genuine Recovery	Edward M. Smith	Alathia Inc. '94
Who Dies	Stephen Levine	Gateway '86
The Courage To Grieve	Judy Tatelbaum	Cedar '95
Tight Corners in Pastoral Counselling	Frank Lake	DLT '81
Consciousness at Birth	David Chamberlain	Chamberlain Com. '92
Father Daughter, Mother Son	Verena Kast	Element '89
Feel The Fear and Do it Anyway	Susan Jeffers	Fawcett, Columbine '88

TO WORK WITH YOUR HANDS
IS TO BE A LABOURER.

TO WORK WITH YOUR HANDS AND YOUR HEAD
IS TO BE AN ARTISAN.

TO WORK WITH YOUR HANDS, HEAD AND HEART
IS TO BE AN ARTIST.

About the Author

Fr. Jim Cogley was born in Wexford in 1954. He trained for the priesthood in St. Patrick's College Maynooth, where he took degrees in English, Philosophy and Theology. Ordained in 1980 for the Diocese of Ferns in Ireland, he has a deep love of the sea and this is reflected in his involvement with the Apostolate of the Sea and in much of his work with symbols. He has spent most of his priesthood in Kilmore Quay, a fishing village in South Wexford. He has many years teaching experience and is a counselling supervisor. As a psychotherapist he trained in the Jungian tradition. His particular area of interest is that of Intergenerational Healing and how the past that is unacknowledged can still influence the present.

His innovative, self-taught, woodturning skills, developed in recent years, provide a unique opportunity to present the age-old truths of life and religion in the form of symbols that speak to the soul. Many of the seminars he conducts throughout the country on topics such as those covered in *Wood You Believe* involve the use of such pieces. Some of his work, that also involves symbols, is the concept of a Memorial Trail and Garden to people lost at sea. Located in Kilmore Quay, this is a major visitor attraction. It incorporates the universal experience of loss and expresses the journey of recovery by combining nautical symbols with the natural landscape of the area.

Wood You Believe, Volume One, *The Unfolding Self* and Volume Two, *The Emerging Self* are his first books to be published. His e-mail address is: *jimcogley@eircom.net*